Acting Up in Church

Humorous sketches for worship services

M. K. Boyle

MERIWETHER PUBLISHING LTD.
Colorado Springs, Colorado

Meriwether Publishing Ltd., Publisher
PO Box 7710
Colorado Springs, CO 80933-7710

Editor: Rhonda Wray
Cover design: Jan Melvin

Library of Congress Cataloging-in-Publication Data

Boyle, M. K., 1961-
Acting up in church : humorous sketches for worship services / by M. K. Boyle.
    p. cm.
Includes index.
ISBN 978-1-56608-109-2 (pbk.)
1. Drama in public worship. 2. Christian drama, American. 3. Comic, The—
Religious aspects—Christianity. 4. Wit and humor—Religious aspects—
Christianity. I. Title.
BV289.B69 2006
246'.72-dc22
                        2006007018

2   3   4   09   10   11

Dedication

To my husband, Jim, for his quick reflexes in vacating the
computer whenever I found the need to write, and to
Reverend Phillip Cameron and the members of Risen Savior
Lutheran church, for laughing in all the right places.

Contents

(All sketches are arranged in alphabetical order for easy reference.)

Preface

I was never a normal child. My sister would walk into the kitchen where our mother was preparing dinner and ask for some sort of refreshment. I, on the other hand, sought more creative measures. I would crawl on my belly, one hand to my throat, the other extended out to my mother, and in the raspiest voice I could muster without causing permanent vocal chord damage, I would cry out, "Water!"

Seeing that I did have a slight flair for the dramatic, it's no wonder I ended up as drama director at an unsuspecting conservative church. The challenge of finding "just the right drama" to match the sermon topic can be compared to finding matching socks in a teenager's room. It's possible, but not without a lot of effort. I discovered I was most appreciative of those sketch books that contained a theme or biblical index. When books or the Internet still did not yield results, I began to write my own material. Nothing gave me more pleasure than when my pastor would ask for a sketch and I was able to write one that matched his sermon topic. One day he approached me and requested a sketch of a certain biblical character. That sounded easy enough ... until he informed me the character was Barabbas!

For days I searched the Internet for any type of drama written about him. I finally concluded that *no one* writes about Barabbas. This was definitely one I was going to have to write myself. I was able to get some background history and speculation about who this man was, but I was still at an impasse regarding what to actually say about it. I finally called my pastor and inquired where he wanted to go with this sermon topic. He said, "I was thinking about how Pilate was deliberating whether Jesus should go free, and how we're often faced with our own debate to follow the world versus Christ." Debate? Instantly I had the idea! "A Cause for Debate" was written that night and performed two days later during the service. I consider that particular sketch one of my most successful, as it really honed in on the theme. It made the pastor's message much more memorable in the minds of the congregation.

1

Occasionally organizations would request a sketch for a special event that would be easy to put together (ten minutes tops) and a lot of fun. "An Adam and Eve Tale" became an instant favorite and has been performed for several youth group activities.

Because most of us don't have a lot of time to memorize, I've created several sketches in which the character carries a prop where his or her lines may be attached. Yes, I confess, we cheat. We've tacked sentences anywhere and everywhere: On clipboards, newspapers, the front of the pew, behind someone's back ... no person or object is safe for the sake of the one-liner.

Because I wanted these sketches to be easy to use, most were created with two to four actors in mind. It is my desire that they will make you laugh, ponder, or smile.

Let the joy of humor be your guide as the Lord directs you in this ministry.

Regards,
M. K. Boyle

An Adam and Eve Tale

Theme: Garden of Eden.

Scripture References: Genesis 2 and 3

Synopsis: A fun exaggeration where a writer recreates the story of Adam and Eve using his/her own words. He/she is unaware that the "characters" have taken a life of their own.

Cast: WRITER
ADAM
EVE

Props: Writing tablet and pencil.

Setting: Writer's office. Place a table or desk and a chair Onstage.

1	*(The WRITER enters and sits at a table Stage Right. He/She picks*
2	*up paper and pen. As the WRITER creates the story, the*
3	*characters of ADAM and EVE are played out in pantomime*
4	*behind him/her. Exaggeration is the key.)*
5	**WRITER:** *(Reading from the paper)* **Create a short anecdote**
6	**regarding the story of Adam and Eve. Hmmm.** *(WRITER*
7	*puts his pen to his mouth, thinks for a minute, and then begins to*
8	*write.)* **There once was a man named Adam.** *(ADAM enters.*
9	*He smiles and points at himself. WRITER pauses and thinks.)* **He**
10	**was very content living in the Garden of Eden. In fact, he**
11	**loved his close association with all the animals and spent**
12	**his days naming them.** *(ADAM points in all directions and*
13	*mouths the words of different animals.)*
14	**But alas, this life of happiness could not go on.** *(ADAM*
15	*freezes his movements. He looks toward the WRITER, confused.)*
16	**Deep in his heart, Adam was lonely.** *(ADAM puts his hand*
17	*to his heart and frowns.)* **In fact, he was forlorn, friendless, a**
18	**veritable desert of desolation.** *(ADAM glances at WRITER*
19	*with a bigger frown. His eyes shift back from the WRITER to the*
20	*audience.)* **In fact, Adam was so lonely, he was besieged to**
21	**the point of despair!** *(ADAM sits on the floor and weeps into*
22	*his hands. WRITER pauses and looks at what is written, then*
23	*starts to erase.)* **No … I don't like that.** *(ADAM looks up from*
24	*his hands.)* **Let's go back to … Adam was lonely.** *(ADAM*
25	*stands and frowns, with his hand to his heart.)* **He longed for a**
26	**companion of his own. So one day he dropped off to**
27	**sleep.** *(ADAM literally drops to the floor. WRITER pauses and*
28	*looks at paper.)* **Wait a minute, that doesn't sound right.**
29	*(ADAM lifts his head and looks at the WRITER, who thinks for a*
30	*second.)* **Adam was walking around the Garden minding**
31	**his own business** *(ADAM stands and starts to walk in a*
32	*nonchalant manner)* **when he suddenly fell asleep.** *(ADAM*
33	*drops to the floor again. WRITER erases paper.)* **No … I don't**
34	**like the way that sounds either.** *(ADAM looks at WRITER in*
35	*confusion.)* **Let's go back to … Adam was sad.** *(ADAM gets*

1   *up and brushes himself off, all the while glaring at the WRITER.*
2   *WRITER is deep in thought as he contemplates what to write*
3   *next.)*
4   God knew it was not good for Adam to be alone, so one
5   day he made him fall into a deep sleep. *(ADAM literally*
6   *falls to the floor again. It looks the same as the previous falls.)*
7   When Adam woke up, *(ADAM gets up)* he stretched,
8   *(Stretches)* he yawned, *(Yawns)* and he thought this day was
9   going to be like all the others. *(He starts to point at all the*
10 *creatures.)* Suddenly, a woman steps out from behind a
11 tree. *(EVE enters. She smiles and points at herself.)* They see
12 each other. *(Both look surprised.)* They wave. *(Both wave*
13 *frantically at each other.)* They run to each other with open
14 arms! *(Arms open, they both run toward each other. WRITER*
15 *looks up.)* **Hold it!** *(ADAM and EVE freeze just inches from each*
16 *other. In this frozen state they maintain their smiles, but their*
17 *eyes look back and forth from audience to WRITER. Again*
18 *WRITER is contemplating what to write next.)* Let's change it
19 to ... They were shy. *(Mime shyness toward each other.)* They
20 were timid ... bashful ... inhibited. *(ADAM and EVE*
21 *continue to act shy, but look at the WRITER as though he is*
22 *weird.)*
23 Then one day, Adam picked Eve up in his arms *(ADAM*
24 *picks up EVE)* and ... and ... *(Stops writing and talks to*
25 *himself.)* Let's see ... If he picks her up, he could walk her
26 to the Garden... *(ADAM starts to struggle)* or show her the
27 animals and the sights ... *(His knees start to shake and buckle)*
28 or they could name the animals together ... *(WRITER starts*
29 *to erase again.)* Oh, I just don't like any of this. I think I'll
30 just drop it. *(ADAM lets go and drops EVE. WRITER starts to*
31 *write again.)*
32 One day Eve came to Adam and presented him with a
33 piece of fruit. *(EVE shows ADAM an imaginary apple.)* Adam
34 recognized it for what it was and immediately rejected it.
35 *(ADAM shakes his head and refuses to take it.)* However, Eve

1   used her womanly charm and persuaded him to eat it.
2   *(EVE shoves the apple into his mouth.)*
3   Suddenly, they both realized they were naked!
4   *(Pantomime modesty by attempting to cover themselves.)* Adam
5   was furious! When God found out, Adam blamed the girl!
6   *(Looks up, points at EVE.)* The consequence for their action
7   was exile from the Paradise Club. *(Both gasp silently.)*
8   Adam was so infuriated, he chased Eve around the
9   Garden. *(ADAM chases EVE in circles.)* When he grabbed
10   her, he put his arms around her throat and he ... he ... *(He*
11   *catches her. [Places thumbs on collarbone – not on actual throat.]*
12   *They freeze. WRITER stops writing and begins to talk to himself.)*
13   Let's see ... What would he do when he actually caught
14   her? *(EVE looks over at the WRITER with arms flailing in an*
15   *effort to get the WRITER to hurry up and finish the sentence.)* I
16   mean, they're already kicked out of the Garden. They've
17   lost favor with God. They'll have to spend the rest of their
18   lives living by the sweat of their brows ... *(ADAM is frozen*
19   *in his stance. She points at her throat, then points at ADAM. She*
20   *mouths the words "Hurry, hurry!")* Besides, that last sentence
21   is not biblically correct, so I'll let it go. *(ADAM releases his*
22   *grip. EVE fans herself. WRITER looks approvingly at his paper.)*
23   Not too bad, if I do say so myself. *(ADAM and EVE high-*
24   *five each other.)* In fact, this was rather fun! Tomorrow I'll
25   write about ... "The Massacre of Sodom and Gomorrah."
26   *(They suddenly freeze and look toward the audience in horror,*
27   *then exit running as if from the WRITER, who also exits.)*

Ask Judy

Theme: Prayer.

**Scripture
References:**   Philippians 4:6, 1 Peter 5:7

Synopsis: A woman seeks advice and is surprised to learn where to turn to for the answers.

Cast: JUDY
SARAH

Props: Optional: A nail file for Judy and a purse to clutch for Sarah.

Setting: Anywhere.

1　　　　*(JUDY stands Center Stage. She's looking quite bored, perhaps*
2　　　　*even filing her nails. Her demeanor and response to questions*
3　　　　*shows the audience she is used to people asking her advice.*
4　　　　*SARAH enters. She is frazzled.)*
5　SARAH: Judy, I have a problem.
6　JUDY: What is it?
7　SARAH: My life seems to be crumbling to pieces. Nothing is
8　　　　going right. I feel out of control!
9　JUDY: Have you tried screaming at the top of your lungs?
10　SARAH: I've already done that.
11　JUDY: What about blaming your husband?
12　SARAH: I did that, too. He wouldn't accept responsibility.
13　JUDY: They never do. What about slamming all the cupboard
14　　　　doors?
15　SARAH: I did that too. I even kicked the refrigerator!
16　JUDY: *(Dismissive wave)* Everybody does that. Have you tried
17　　　　praying?
18　SARAH: Tried what?
19　JUDY: You know — get down on your knees and ask God to
20　　　　"help you" kind of praying?
21　SARAH: I've got bad knees.
22　JUDY: Sitting or standing is just as effective.
23　SARAH: Well, I don't know. Are you sure there isn't anything
24　　　　I could *destroy* before trying that?
25　JUDY: Trust me, it's a lot less stressful.
26　SARAH: How can that be?
27　JUDY: Jesus promises to be with us. He promises to hear our
28　　　　prayers. By trusting in him, we know he has our best
29　　　　interest in mind. We don't have to worry because we
30　　　　know he's in control.
31　SARAH: It's a lot more fun to blame my husband.
32　JUDY: I know. You'll get over it.
33　SARAH: Isn't it sort of a last-ditch effort?
34　JUDY: Usually is for most people. What do you have to lose?
35　SARAH: I *have* used up all my other resources. OK, I'll try it.

1   *(Starts to exit.)* **Now I lay me down to sleep.** *(Stops and turns*
2   *to JUDY.)* **Is that an appropriate prayer?**
3 **JUDY: We all have to start with the basics.** *(They exit.)*

Ask Judy Again

Theme:	Resolving conflicts with prayer.
Scripture References:	Matthew 18:20, James 4:1-3
Synopsis:	A teenager comes to Judy for advice about problems with his/her parents.
Cast:	JUDY TEEN
Props:	A nail file for Judy.
Setting:	Anywhere.

1   *(JUDY stands Center Stage. She is filing her nails and looking*
2   *bored as usual. The TEEN approaches.)*
3   TEEN: Judy, I need your help. My life is falling apart!
4   JUDY: *(Doesn't look up and continues to file nails.)* **Again?**
5   TEEN: But this time it's serious!
6   JUDY: Problems with parents?
7   TEEN: In the worst way. They won't give me a car, they put me
8   on a curfew, and then they blocked the minutes on my cell
9   phone.
10 JUDY: Hmmm. Sounds frustrating.
11 TEEN: Totally! I'm going nuts. They treat me like a child!
12 JUDY: Have you tried throwing a tantrum?
13 TEEN: Oh yeah, that's the first thing I did. Full-blown ... on
14   the floor ... kicking and screaming.
15 JUDY: What about yelling at them? Telling them they don't
16   understand you?
17 TEEN: No effect. All they did was roll their eyes. *(TEEN rolls*
18   *his/her eyes in an exaggerated motion.)*
19 JUDY: What about threatening to move out?
20 TEEN: *(Bitter)* I did that too. *(Addresses the audience.)* **They got**
21   *way* too happy.
22 JUDY: Have you tried praying with them?
23 TEEN: *(Taken aback)* I ... I can't do that. They're the enemy!
24 JUDY: You'd be surprised how conflicts are resolved when
25   people come together in this way.
26 TEEN: But that would mean actually being in the room with
27   them. That can't solve anything except more fighting.
28 JUDY: Prayer does more than you think. God's word can
29   transform lives, heal hurts, clear up disagreements,
30   impart joy, give strength, fulfill hope, and release power.
31 TEEN: *(Lights up.)* How much power?
32 JUDY: The point is, when conflicts are resolved through
33   prayer, sometimes you're able to come up with a solution
34   to the problem.
35 TEEN: You mean like buying me a new car?

1   JUDY: Or granting more time with the family car.
2   TEEN: I knew there was a catch. *(Thinks for a second.)* **What if I**
3   **tried slamming a few doors first?** *(JUDY gives TEEN a*
4   *"look.")* **Oh, all right! I guess I'll just have to take that big**
5   **step and try to resolve this like an adult.**
6   JUDY: I'm sure your parents will be relieved. *(They exit.)*

The Bad Attitudes

Theme: The Beatitudes, humility, and the Christian attitude.

Scripture Reference: Matthew 5:2-6

Synopsis: A member of the Secret Service misinterprets the meaning of the Sermon on the Mount.

Cast: SECRET SERVICE AGENT
SPEAKER
2-4 EXTRA SECRET SERVICE ASSISTANTS (Non-speaking parts)

Costumes: Dark suits and sunglasses for the Secret Service Agents.

Props: Note pad.

Setting: Your local church.

1   *(The SPEAKER stands Center Stage.)*
2   **SPEAKER: Today's lesson is on Matthew chapter five …**
3   **SECRET SERVICE AGENT:** *(Stands up.)* **Hold it! Secure the**
4   **entrances.** *(Several SECRET SERVICE ASSISTANTS station*
5   *themselves at the front of the stage and along the aisles. The SECRET*
6   *SERVICE AGENT walks up to the SPEAKER.)*
7   **SPEAKER: What is going on here?**
8   **SECRET SERVICE AGENT: I'll be the one to ask the questions.**
9   **SPEAKER: Who are you?**
10   **SECRET SERVICE AGENT: The Secret Service.**
11   **SPEAKER: You have no right to interrupt this service!**
12   **SECRET SERVICE AGENT: WE have every right. We are**
13   **authorized to investigate any suspicious or deviant characters**
14   **appropriated in the _____** *(Insert your denomination)*
15   **church.**
16   **SPEAKER: But we're just average people!**
17   **SECRET SERVICE AGENT: Not according to our records.** *(Pulls*
18   *out a note pad.)* **For the past twelve months, there's been a high**
19   **turnover of …** *(Reads from his notes.)* **poor sports, cry babies,**
20   **pushovers, and gluttons.**
21   **SPEAKER: Nobody's perfect. We all have faults …**
22   **SECRET SERVICE AGENT:** *(Interrupts.)* **Not in the Secret Service,**
23   **buddy! We're under strict orders to remain perfect at all**
24   **times.**
25   **SPEAKER: Ooookay …**
26   **SECRET SERVICE AGENT: Normally these character flaws**
27   **would be considered desirable, even preferable, during**
28   **interrogations. However, we have come to learn that this**
29   **church rewards such behavior.**
30   **SPEAKER: Rewards? In what way?**
31   **SECRET SERVICE AGENT: All right … you want to play**
32   **ignorant? We can play that game too.** *(Shows note pad.)* **It says**
33   **right here, "Blessed are the poor sports, for theirs is the**
34   **kingdom of heaven." Pretty nice rewards for a bunch of**
35   *losers,* **wouldn't you say?**

1   SPEAKER: That's "poor in spirit"! "Blessed are the poor in spirit,
2   for theirs is the kingdom of heaven" (Matthew 5:3).
3   SECRET SERVICE AGENT: Don't try to change the wording,
4   buddy. We got this information right from your own Bible
5   under the subheading, "Bad Attitudes."
6   SPEAKER: That's Beatitudes!
7   SECRET SERVICE AGENT: *(Ignoring him)* There's a whole section
8   we decoded to uncover this church's *true* agenda.
9   SPEAKER: *(Looking in Bible)* There's a lot of good counsel in here.
10   "Blessed are those who mourn..."
11   SECRET SERVICE AGENT: Cry babies.
12   SPEAKER: "The meek....."
13   SECRET SERVICE AGENT: Pushovers.
14   SPEAKER: "Those who hunger and thirst for righteousness ..."
15   SECRET SERVICE AGENT: *(Disgustedly)* Gluttons.
16   SPEAKER: Look, all these attitudes actually take courage! We
17   have a saying in this church: "In order to come to Christ, you
18   have to first start on your knees." I mean, haven't you ever
19   humbled yourself in that way? *(SECRET SERVICE AGENT*
20   *slowly looks toward the SPEAKER, arms crossed.)* OK. Let me
21   rephrase that.
22   SECRET SERVICE AGENT: I'll tell you what I'm going to do. I'm
23   going to let you off the hook. Your ideas may be misguided,
24   but I believe they're sincere. Who knows? Maybe this lowly
25   attitude concept will work.
26   SPEAKER: You're very kind.
27   SECRET SERVICE AGENT: Now is not the time to be insulting,
28   buddy — I'm cutting you a break.
29   SPEAKER: Sorry.
30   SECRET SERVICE AGENT: Just remember, we're watching you.
31   *(Nods at other SECRET SERVICE ASSISTANTS, and they all exit.)*
32   SPEAKER: Wow. *(Pause)* Blessed are the arrogant, for they make
33   the rest of us look good! *(Exits.)*

The *Bored* Room

Theme: Lukewarm Christians, hypocrites.

Scripture Reference: Revelation 3:15-16

Synopsis: In this spoof of the TV show, *The Apprentice*, three apprentices must face the "bored" room and report the results of their assignment.

Cast: TRUMPET
BLOW HORN
DRY MOSS
NAVEL LINT
ROTTEN WOOD

Costumes: Business attire.

Props: One to three clipboards.

Setting: Somewhere "down there." Place a table and two chairs at Center Stage.

1   (*MR. TRUMPET is sitting at a table. Enter BLOW HORN.*)
2 **BLOW HORN: The apprentices are ready to enter the bored**
3   **room, Mr. Trumpet.**
4 **TRUMPET: Excellent. Send them in.** (*BLOW HORN waves DRY*
5   *MOSS, NAVEL LINT, and ROTTEN WOOD in. They enter*
6   *and line up single file. TRUMPET addresses the first one.*) **Tell**
7   **me, Miss ...** (*Looks down at clipboard.*)
8 **DRY MOSS: Dry Moss, sir.**
9 **TRUMPET: Tell me, Dry Moss, why do you want to work for**
10   **me?**
11 **DRY MOSS: Oh, I think you're wonderful, Mr. Trumpet. I've**
12   **studied every tactic you used to get Christians to fall away**
13   **from their faith.**
14 **TRUMPET:** (*Unimpressed. Doesn't look up but continues to flip*
15   *through the clipboard.*) **Uh-huh. Mr. Blow Horn, it says here**
16   **that in Dry Moss's last assignment, she only managed to**
17   **get three individuals to stumble from their faith.**
18 **BLOW HORN: That is correct, Mr. Trumpet.**
19 **TRUMPET:** (*Looks up at DRY MOSS.*) **Three people? That's**
20   **terrible, Dry Moss. How can you account for such a poor**
21   **showing?**
22 **DRY MOSS:** (*Getting nervous*) **Well ... uh, it was really** *hard*, **Mr.**
23   **Trumpet. I tried to voice doubt in their ears, but they**
24   **wouldn't listen.**
25 **TRUMPET: But only three believers?**
26 **BLOW HORN: Technically, they're not even believers. Only**
27   **visitors.**
28 **DRY MOSS:** (*Trying to sound enthused*) **It was really easy, too. I**
29   **just pointed out how ridiculous everyone looked with**
30   **their arms raised and ...**
31 **TRUMPET:** (*To BLOW HORN*) **Arms raised?**
32 **BLOW HORN: In prayer.**
33 **TRUMPET: In prayer! Don't you know you can't attack while**
34   **people are praying? Have you learned** *nothing* **from my**
35   **books?** (*The other two APPRENTICES snicker.*)

1 DRY MOSS: But they were all so young in their faith, I
2   thought they'd fall like flies at the slightest signs of
3   doubt.
4 TRUMPET: Miss Dry Moss, why do you think we call this the
5   "bored room"?
6 DRY MOSS: I — I'm not sure.
7 TRUMPET: In our department, we're not actually trying to get
8   Christians to reject their faith. We have a better plan than
9   that. We want them to get bored. A bored Christian is an
10   ineffective Christian. They're fence walkers!
11 BLOW HORN: Yeah, and that really ticks off the Big Guy.
12 TRUMPET: You targeted praying, spirit-filled Christians. That
13   means they're excited about their faith. You failed in your
14   mission. You're fired.
15 DRY MOSS: Oh, man! *(Exits, dejected.)*
16 TRUMPET: *(Turns to next apprentice.)* And who are you?
17 NAVEL LINT: *(Scared, whiny voice)* Navel Lint, sir.
18 TRUMPET: And why do you want to work for me, Navel Lint?
19 NAVEL LINT: Well, um, M — Mr. Trumpet, I sort of repel
20   people by my presence, so I think I would be good for
21   your company.
22 TRUMPET: *(Flipping through clipboard)* Uh-huh. According to
23   your stats, you didn't do the job assigned to you.
24 NAVEL LINT: I did! I mean, I wasn't stupid enough to attack
25   them when they were praying or singing, Mr. Trumpet.
26 TRUMPET: So what kind of church did you pick?
27 NAVEL LINT: A boring one! I mean, the Pastor was so dull that
28   even I started to nod off. By the end of the hour, I had well
29   over half of them yawning or falling asleep.
30 TRUMPET: So you made a bunch of them unusually tired. Is
31   that all you have to offer me? How many fence walkers?
32   *(NAVEL LINT stammers. TRUMPET looks over at BLOW*
33   *HORN.)*
34 BLOW HORN: None.
35 TRUMPET: None! *(To NAVEL LINT)* Not one? How can you

1   account for that?
2   BLOW HORN: He picked a conservative church. *(TRUMPET*
3   *shakes his head.)*
4   NAVEL LINT: What does that mean?
5   TRUMPET: It means you did *nothing* to turn them into
6   hypocrites.
7   BLOW HORN: The best you did was give them a good nap.
8   TRUMPET: It doesn't matter to these Christians if the speaker
9   is dull. They tend to find ways to grow through Scripture
10   readings or songs or anything else in the service. *(Points at*
11   *NAVEL LINT.)* You failed in your mission. You're fired.
12   *(NAVEL LINT leaves, head bowed and dejected. TRUMPET*
13   *turns to next APPRENTICE.)* And your name?
14   ROTTEN WOOD: Rotten Wood, sir.
15   TRUMPET: Why do you want to work for me, Rotten Wood?
16   ROTTEN WOOD: *(Cocky)* Because you need me.
17   TRUMPET: *(Surprised)* Excuse me?
18   BLOW HORN: His numbers are impressive, Mr. Trumpet.
19   TRUMPET: *(Looking through clipboard)* It says here that none of
20   your charges left the church.
21   ROTTEN WOOD: I didn't *want* them to leave the church.
22   TRUMPET: Well, what kind of church did you pick?
23   ROTTEN WOOD: *(Makes a sound of disgust.)* I don't step into
24   those places.
25   BLOW HORN: *(To TRUMPET)* If you look on page two, you'll
26   see the number of people who want nothing to do with
27   the church or Christianity in general. *(TRUMPET flips over*
28   *to the page.)*
29   TRUMPET: Two hundred and fifty-seven!
30   ROTTEN WOOD: It would have been more, but I did the best
31   I could with the time schedule you gave me.
32   TRUMPET: How did you do it?
33   ROTTEN WOOD: It's easy, once you know their weaknesses.
34   The Meyers family, for example, are known to shout
35   obscenities during sports events. I simply let it be known

1   among the others that this family confesses to be
2   Christians. I was able to repel an entire bench section
3   away from church simply on the basis of this family's
4   attitude.
5   TRUMPET: *(Impressed)* Amazing.
6   ROTTEN WOOD: Then there is Rob Peterson. He carries his
7   Bible to classes so everyone can marvel at how religious
8   he is. What they don't know is that he has a desire to be
9   "one of the guys." So I hooked him up with several
10   people who see him act one way with his church friends,
11   but another way with them. They like this guy, but
12   obviously the church has nothing special to offer *them,* so
13   they stay away from any invitations to get to know Christ.
14   BLOW HORN: Now that's what I call *true* fence walkers. No
15   wonder the Big Guy says he's going to "spit them out of
16   his mouth" (Revelation 3:16, author's paraphrase).
17   TRUMPET: And Rotten Wood here knows that lukewarm
18   Christians repel those looking for truth and light. We
19   need more men like him. *(Turns to ROTTEN WOOD.)*
20   You're hired!
21   ROTTEN WOOD: Thank you, Mr. Trumpet. *(They all shake*
22   *hands and exit.)*

Brotherly Love

Theme: Sermon on the Mount, love.

**Scripture
Reference:**   Matthew 5:22

Synopsis: The "Sons of Thunder" learn a lesson in love.

Cast: JAMES
JOHN
WOMAN
VOICE (Off-stage)

Costumes: Biblical robes.

Props: None.

Setting: Sitting in a crowd, listening to the Sermon on the Mount.

1   *(JAMES, JOHN, and a WOMAN sit shoulder to shoulder, very*
2   *close to one another. Extras may be added for more effect.)*
3   **JAMES: John, will you move away and give me some space?**
4   **JOHN: You're the one touching me!**
5   **JAMES: There you go, whining again.**
6   **JOHN: James, I am *not* whining! It's so crowded here I can**
7   **barely move!**
8   **WOMAN: Shhh. I'm trying to hear what the Master is saying.**
9   **JAMES: Stop getting us in trouble.**
10 **JOHN: Me? You're the reason Dad called us the "Sons of**
11 **Thunder."**
12 **JAMES: No it wasn't, it was your big mouth!**
13 **JOHN: My mouth!**
14 **WOMAN: *(More forceful this time)* Shhh!**
15 **JAMES: You were always Mom's favorite.**
16 **JOHN: *(Slight chuckle)* Yeah. *(Quickly recovers.)* I mean ... You're**
17 **exaggerating.**
18 **JAMES: Are you calling me a liar?**
19 **JOHN: No, I'm calling you *stupid*.**
20 **JAMES: You want to take that outside?**
21 **JOHN: We *are* outside, you airhead.**
22 **JAMES: And you're an idiot.**
23 **JOHN: *(Raises fists.)* Oh, yeah?**
24 **JAMES: *(Counters the move.)* Yeah!**
25 **WOMAN: Shhh! *(Both immediately drop their fists.)***
26 **VOICE: *(From Off-stage)* But I tell you, anyone who is angry**
27 **with his brother must answer for it in court. Anyone who**
28 **calls his brother "empty-headed" is in danger of going to**
29 **the highest court. Anyone who calls him a fool is in**
30 **danger of hellfire ...**
31 **JOHN: Court?**
32 **JAMES: Hellfire? *(Both look at each other, then spontaneously***
33 *engage in a side embrace.)*
34 **JOHN: I love you, brother.**
35 **JAMES: Me too, brother. I didn't mean what I said.**

1   JOHN: Neither did I. You're a wonderful big brother. *(Pause)*
2   Even if you *are* bossy.
3   JAMES: And you've always been the perfect little brother. All
4   that kissing up and tattling never did bother me ... much.
5   JOHN: It's a good thing we love each other so much.
6   Otherwise I could barely stand to be next to you.
7   JAMES: You got *that* right.
8   WOMAN: *(Looks at both of them with disgust, then turns to the*
9   *audience.)* I don't know about you, but I liked them better
10   when they were fighting.
11   JAMES: So ... just between the two of us, Jesus loves *me* best.
12   JOHN: What?! *(All characters freeze. Blackout.)*

A Call to Retreat

Theme: Marriage.

Scripture Reference: 1 Corinthians 13

Synopsis: A lighthearted sketch using the theme of *The Honeymooners* to promote a marriage retreat.

Cast: ROLPH
ALLY
NEWMAN
TRUDY
SALESPERSON

Costumes: Retro clothing, if desired.

Props: Spray bottle full of water that says "Grouch-Be-Gone."

Setting: Rolph and Ally's home. Place a table and chairs at Center Stage.

1   *(Play the theme from* The Honeymooners, *if available. ROLPH*
2   *enters.)*
3   **ROLPH: Ally? I'm home!** *(Opens his arms as if to expect his wife to*
4   *embrace him. Nothing. He looks around, opens his arms, and*
5   *announces again)* **Ally, I'm home!** *(Still nothing. This time he*
6   *drops his arms and says more forcefully)* **Ally!**
7   **ALLY:** *(Off-stage)* **In a minute!** *(ROLPH walks over to the table and*
8   *looks at it in disbelief. ALLY enters.)* **Now what are you**
9   **bellyaching about?**
10   **ROLPH:** *(Points at the table.)* **Do you see something wrong here?**
11   **ALLY: Yeah. You promised to replace that crummy old table**
12   **two years ago.**
13   **ROLPH: But there's something** *missing* **on this "crummy"**
14   **table that should be here when I come home from work.**
15   *(Looks for ALLY to respond. ALLY just stands there and says*
16   *nothing. ROLPH is clearly frustrated.)* **My dinner, Ally.**
17   **Where is my dinner?**
18   **ALLY:** *(Unconcerned)* **Oh, that. I was busy, OK?**
19   **ROLPH:** *(Disbelieving) You* **were busy …**
20   **ALLY:** *(Irritated)* **Yes, I was busy! You got a problem with that?!**
21   **ROLPH: A man comes home after a hard day's work, he**
22   **expects his "loving wife" to greet him at the door with his**
23   **dinner on the table.**
24   **ALLY: You drive a bus all day. You've never worked a hard day**
25   **in your life.**
26   **ROLPH: Don't start with me, Ally. You don't have to deal with**
27   **the smog or the crabby passengers or the …**
28   **ALLY: No, I just deal with a crabby husband.**
29   **ROLPH: One of these days, Ally, one of these days … pow! To**
30   **the moon!**
31   **ALLY: Did it ever occur to you to ask me how** *my* **day went?**
32   **ROLPH:** *Your* **day? You don't** *do* **anything important.**
33   **ALLY: Exactly. I'm tired of sitting around in this bug-infested**
34   **apartment. The furniture is outdated, the cabinets are in**
35   **need of repair, and you don't make enough money for me**

1   to join a gym or take classes, so ... *(Pause)* I went looking
2   for a job.
3   ROLPH: *(Disbelieving/critical)* A job ...
4   ALLY: Yes, a job. *(NEWMAN and TRUDY enter.)*
5   NEWMAN: Hi ya, Rolph.
6   TRUDY: Hi Rolph, hi Ally.
7   ALLY: Hi, Trudy.
8   ROLPH: Guess what, Newman? Ally went looking for a job
9   today.
10   NEWMAN: Yes, I know. How'd it go, Ally?
11   ROLPH: You knew?
12   NEWMAN: Sure! Trudy went too.
13   ROLPH: *(Grabs NEWMAN and pulls him over to the side.)*
14   Newman! The reason why they're looking for a job is
15   because they don't think we can take care of them.
16   NEWMAN: I don't see it that way, Rolph.
17   ROLPH: *(Points at the table.)* Do you see that empty table there?
18   NEWMAN: Yeah.
19   ROLPH: There is *no* dinner on that table. This is what's going
20   to happen to you if Trudy gets a job.
21   NEWMAN: You get dinner?
22   ROLPH: *(Surprised)* Sure ... every night. Don't you?
23   TRUDY: *(Waves it off.)* Dinner is overrated.
24   NEWMAN: *(To TRUDY)* Hey, if you get a job, I want to start
25   eating in the evenings.
26   TRUDY: You've got two hands, fix it yourself. Besides, I plan
27   to work evenings.
28   ALLY: But Trudy, then you'd never see each other.
29   TRUDY: At least I won't have to smell him when he gets home.
30   He works all day at the sewer, and he never bathes!
31   ALLY: I know what you mean. Rolph smells like gasoline.
32   NEWMAN: *(Sniffs his underarms.)* What's wrong with the way I
33   smell?
34   ROLPH: Oh, you know women. If you don't smell like a
35   petunia, they think something's wrong with you. *(The next*

1   *four lines quickly overlap each other.)*

2   **ALLY:** Now you see here, Rolph.

3   **ROLPH:** No, you see *here*, Ally.

4   **NEWMAN:** I think I deserve to be fed.

5   **TRUDY:** In your dreams ... *(All start arguing at once. Commercial*
6   *SALESPERSON enters Stage Right. She/he holds up a spray*
7   *bottle and addresses the audience. The arguing couples decrease*
8   *their volume so only the commercial is heard. ROLPH and*
9   *NEWMAN continue to mouth words to themselves while ALLY*
10   *and TRUDY suddenly become interested in the commercial's*
11   *words.)*

12   **SALESPERSON:** This could happen to you. You're on the road
13   of life, and you've suddenly become aware that your
14   marriage is no honeymoon. What do you do?

15   The answer is simple. For only twenty-two ninety-
16   nine, you can change your spouse from a grouchy,
17   miserable, overbearing person to one who is attentive,
18   caring, and considerate. That's right! Just a spray of
19   "Grouch-Be-Gone" can transform your lives!

20   No longer will your husband complain of a late dinner.
21   One spray of this, *(Sprays can)* and he'll thank you for
22   controlling his weight problem. Having problems with
23   your nagging wife? One spray of this, and ... *Hey*! *(ALLY*
24   *and TRUDY sneak up to the SALESPERSON and grab the can.*
25   *They then run over to ROLPH and NEWMAN and spray them*
26   *too.)*

27   **NEWMAN:** Hey, cut it out!

28   **ROLPH:** What are you doing? Have you lost your minds?
29   *(ALLY and TRUDY look at each other in confusion, giving the*
30   *SALESPERSON time to snatch back the spray can.)*

31   **ALLY:** But ... we ... thought ...

32   **SALESPERSON:** Did you honestly think a spray bottle full of
33   water would solve your problems? What do you think
34   marriage retreats are for? Sheeeesh! *(All watch*
35   *SALESPERSON exit, then they exit also.)*

Camping in the Valley

Theme: Difficulty, fear, trials.

**Scripture
Reference:** Psalm 23

Synopsis: A despondent man walking through the "trials of life" finds someone who has the solution to facing hard times. Or does he?

Cast: PETER
DAVE

Props: A fishing pole, a cup, a walking stick. A rope with a piece of tarp thrown across it could be used as a makeshift tent for effect.

Setting: A campsite. Place two chairs at Center Stage and hang up a sign that says, "Shadow Valley." Below this sign should be three "one way arrow" signs that say, "Hard Times," "Difficult Times," and "Total Ruin."

1   *(PETER sits Center Stage holding his fishing pole.)*
2   PETER: *(Singing)* **Nobody knows the trouble I've seen.**
3   **Nobody knows my sorrow.** *(DAVE enters.)*
4   DAVE: **Hey, brother, could you spare a cup of cold water?**
5   PETER: **Certainly! I'm always willing to help a fellow man in**
6   **need. These are tough times we're facing.** *(Hands him a*
7   *cup.)*
8   DAVE: **It sure is.** *(He takes the cup and sits down.)* **Thank you.**
9   PETER: **So, friend, what brings you to "the valley of the**
10   **shadow of death"?**
11   DAVE: **What did you call this place?**
12   PETER: **Surely you knew the twenty-third psalm is an actual**
13   **location!**
14   DAVE: **Well ... I ... uh ...**
15   PETER: *(Quoting from memory)* **"Yea, though I walk through the**
16   **valley of the shadow of death, I will fear no evil: for thou**
17   **art with me"** (Psalm 23:4).
18   DAVE: **You ... you mean I'm dead?**
19   PETER: **Of course not! Death takes on many forms. Death of a**
20   **loved one, loss of a job, end of a relationship ... you**
21   **know, things like that.**
22   DAVE: **Well, I've certainly been going through some hard**
23   **times.**
24   PETER: **Yes, I know.**
25   DAVE: **You do?**
26   PETER: **Sure. Otherwise you wouldn't be here.**
27   DAVE: **My name's Dave.** *(DAVE extends his hand. PETER accepts*
28   *the gesture, and they shake hands.)*
29   PETER: **Peter. I'm a fisherman.**
30   DAVE: **Oh? Catch anything?**
31   PETER: **Haven't had so much as a nibble in ...** *(Thinks for a*
32   *second)* **oh ... about fifteen years now.**
33   DAVE: **Fifteen years? You've been here that long?**
34   PETER: **Sure enough.**
35   DAVE: **What happened?**

1   PETER: Well, I lost my business to bad financial investments,
2   and then shortly after that I lost my wife.
3   DAVE: Oh, did she die?
4   PETER: Nope. Wandered off in the amusement park. Haven't
5   seen her since.
6   DAVE: Didn't you go looking for her?
7   PETER: Of course. But with my world closing in on me, I
8   found myself here. *(Spreads his arms.)* So I figure I'll just
9   stay awhile.
10   DAVE: So ... you've been camping in your sorrows for fifteen
11   years?
12   PETER: I've made a comfortable home here.
13   DAVE: It's kind of lonely.
14   PETER: It's safe, and I don't have to worry about taking risks.
15   DAVE: What risks are you afraid of?
16   PETER: Everything! If I make an attempt at another business, I
17   might fail.
18   DAVE: You might succeed.
19   PETER: If I give someone my heart, they might crush it.
20   DAVE: Then again, you may find love.
21   PETER: If I tell someone my dreams, I may get laughed at.
22   DAVE: Or you may find support.
23   PETER: *(Irritated)* Are you always this cheery?
24   DAVE: Not usually, no.
25   PETER: Then how can you offer words of encouragement
26   when you yourself are at a low point?
27   DAVE: *(Shrugs.)* I don't know. Maybe it was the Bible passage
28   you quoted. The Lord said he would be with us through
29   the valley of death. I guess it gave me a little hope. *(Pause)*
30   Perhaps I can find some comfort in those words through
31   my journey.
32   PETER: Comfort? I have just the thing you need. *(Reaches down*
33   *and pulls up a walking stick.)*
34   DAVE: A stick?
35   PETER: It's not just a stick. It's a staff! You know, for walking.

1   *(DAVE looks puzzled at the staff. PETER sighs.)* **Don't you**
2   **remember the rest of the verse? "Thy rod and thy staff**
3   **they comfort me"** (Psalm 23:4). **I've got the rod.** *(Holds up*
4   *the fishing pole.)* **You can have the staff.**
5   DAVE: **Don't you need it?**
6   PETER: **It hasn't helped me much. I've gotten more use out of**
7   **the rod.**
8   DAVE: **But you haven't caught anything!**
9   PETER: **So what's your point?**
10   DAVE: **Look.** *(DAVE stands and looks down the road.)* **We've got**
11   **his rod and his staff. He says he will be with us and**
12   **comfort us. Come with me. Let's walk out of this valley.**
13   PETER: **I ... don't know. It's kind of hazy and uncertain in the**
14   **distance.**
15   DAVE: **But we'll never see the new light of day until we take**
16   **the steps of faith. Come on. Do you want to sit here the**
17   **rest of your life?**
18   PETER: *(Pause)* **Perhaps it wouldn't hurt to try.** *(PETER stands.)*
19   **I'm a little rusty with this.**
20   DAVE: **It's all right. The Lord is with us.** *(Both exit.)*

A Cause for Debate

Theme: Personal commitment, making a choice.

**Scripture
References:**   Matthew 27:15-26; Luke 23:25

Synopsis: Opponents face off in a debate to convince the masses who they should follow: Christ with salvation, or Barabbas with the world.

Cast: (Male or female)
MEDIATOR
DEBATER FOR CHRIST
DEBATER FOR BARABBAS

Props: None.

Setting: A debate. The Debaters may use podiums if desired.

1   *(The DEBATERS stand on opposite ends of the stage. For effect,*
2   *several people may be sitting just under the stage and respond to*
3   *each point of the debate by clapping, booing, or cheering. For*
4   *smaller groups, audience participation is not required. The*
5   *MEDIATOR is standing Center Stage. He/she sets up the debate,*
6   *then exits.)*
7   **MEDIATOR: As is customary during this time of Passover, a**
8   **prisoner is released from Roman custody. We have two**
9   **men with two different crimes: Jesus Barabbas and Jesus**
10   **of Nazareth. Representatives from each side will debate**
11   **their cause while presenting their appeals to the public.**
12   **_____** *(Insert name of DEBATER FOR BARABBAS)* **will**
13   **argue the cause of Barabbas, while _____** *(Insert*
14   *name of DEBATER FOR CHRIST)* **will argue the cause of**
15   **Jesus. Ladies,** *(or Gentlemen)* **I turn the floor to you.**
16   *(MEDIATOR exits.)*
17   **DEBATER FOR CHRIST: Thank you. As you know, Jesus has**
18   **done many wonderful things for his people ...**
19   **DEBATER FOR BARABBAS: What's so wonderful about him?**
20   **He goes around talking! That's all he does is talk, talk,**
21   **talk. What we need is a man of action!**
22   **DEBATER FOR CHRIST: Don't forget that Jesus performed**
23   **many miracles. He healed the sick. He raised Lazarus**
24   **from the dead! Barabbas's only "action" was to plunder**
25   **and steal in the name of his cause.**
26   **DEBATER FOR BARABBAS: He only did what any one of you**
27   **would do to make a better life for himself and everyone**
28   **here. Do you all want to remain subjects of the Romans?**
29   **Do you want to pay taxes to them and worship their gods?**
30   **And as long as we're talking crimes, what about Jesus'**
31   **crimes?**
32   **DEBATER FOR CHRIST: Jesus never committed any crimes.**
33   **He was a model citizen ...**
34   **DEBATER FOR BARABBAS: A model citizen to the Romans.**
35   **DEBATER FOR CHRIST: He's an example to all of us of how**

1   to live a God-pleasing life. He showed us kindness. He
2   wasn't a thief like Barabbas.
3   DEBATER FOR BARABBAS: Hey, it's not his fault he's not
4   rich like some of you. The tax collectors took all his
5   money, leaving his family to starve! Jesus hangs out with
6   tax collectors — the very people who service the people
7   we hate! Are we going to stand for this?
8   DEBATER FOR CHRIST: Don't forget that Barabbas is a
9   murderer as well. That's worse than a tax collector. Jesus
10   teaches about love.
11   DEBATER FOR BARABBAS: It's not murder when it's war!
12   Barabbas is willing to fight for his beliefs. He's willing to
13   lay his life down for his cause. Why isn't Jesus willing to
14   fight for *his* cause?
15   DEBATER FOR CHRIST: Jesus teaches about compassion and
16   getting along with other people. He teaches about the
17   kingdom of heaven. That is his cause.
18   DEBATER FOR BARABBAS: He claims to be the Son of God!
19   That's not a cause, that's heresy!
20   DEBATERS FOR CHRIST and BARABBAS: *(Point at each other*
21   *and say in unison.)* **His crimes are punishable by death!**
22   *(Both pause and look at each other, still pointing. Finally they*
23   *compose themselves again.)*
24   DEBATER FOR CHRIST: If you follow Jesus, he will set you
25   free from the worry and hate.
26   DEBATER FOR BARABBAS: If you follow Barabbas, he will
27   set you free from everything we have known to cause
28   hate.
29   DEBATER FOR CHRIST: Follow him, and he will make you
30   fishers of men.
31   DEBATER FOR BARABBAS: Follow him, and he will make
32   you conquerors of men.
33   DEBATER FOR CHRIST: Only through Jesus can you find
34   peace.
35   DEBATER FOR BARABBAS: Only by fighting can you

1   demand peace. Choose Barabbas.
2   **DEBATER FOR CHRIST:** Choose Jesus.
3   **DEBATER FOR BARABBAS:** Choose Barabbas!
4   **DEBATER FOR CHRIST:** Choose Jesus! *(MEDIATOR enters.)*
5   **MEDIATOR:** Thank you, ladies *(or Gentlemen). (Turns to*
6   *audience.)* **And now the choice is yours. Do you follow the**
7   **son of a rabbi, or the son of a carpenter? The thief or the**
8   **heretic? We now leave it to the people.** *(All exit.)*

Deciphering the Good

Theme: Judging others, evangelism.

**Scripture
References:**   Matthew 9:9-13, Romans 14:10

Synopsis: Two women take a "Pharisee" point of view when evaluating those in need of evangelizing.

Cast: NAOMI
CLAIRE

Props: None.

Setting: At church.

1   *(NAOMI stands Center Stage. CLAIRE walks up.)*
2   CLAIRE: Naomi, good morning!
3   NAOMI: Claire! Good morning to you too. It's a beautiful
4   Sunday, isn't it?
5   CLAIRE: Yes, it is. I heard you've joined our evangelism
6   committee.
7   NAOMI: I have. I'm really excited about meeting new people
8   and sharing the gospel.
9   CLAIRE: Oh yes, this church could always use good people.
10   Take Charles Edelmister, for example. He's a corporate
11   executive. Very important. We snatched him away from
12   the "First Church of Ultimate Lethargy."
13   NAOMI: The Irbeys are new too, aren't they?
14   CLAIRE: Ricardo and Mona. They're missionaries ... or at
15   least they were until they found out they'd have to travel.
16   NAOMI: Who's that talking to Mona?
17   CLAIRE: *(Disgusted)* Oh, her. That's Dolores Dunderhall's
18   daughter. I can't believe she had the nerve to show up
19   here.
20   NAOMI: She looks like she's about to go into labor at any
21   minute.
22   CLAIRE: If I was Dolores, I wouldn't have brought her here. I
23   mean, it's bad enough that she's not even married.
24   NAOMI: I'd be afraid to even talk to her. People might see me
25   and think that I approve of the situation.
26   CLAIRE: Exactly. Oh look, there's Guire Krogan! He just got
27   out of prison you know.
28   NAOMI: What for?
29   CLAIRE: I think he stole some money from his employer.
30   NAOMI: And he got caught? He wasn't very good at it, was he!
31   CLAIRE: They say he's repented, but I don't believe it. I once
32   tested him by placing a twenty dollar bill on the
33   secretary's desk. I then asked him to get something out of
34   the office. When I went back in to check, the money was
35   gone!

1 NAOMI: Was this twenty dollar bill lying on the far right
2   corner next to the Good News Bible?
3 CLAIRE: Yes. How did you know?
4 NAOMI: *(Quickly)* **No reason!** *(Looks around quickly to see if*
5   *anyone has heard their conversation.)*
6 CLAIRE: Oh look, there's Wynona Whipple. Stay away from
7   her, she's got anger issues. And over there is Peter
8   Ashbury. He's been an embarrassment ever since he got
9   mixed up with "you-know-who."
10 NAOMI: Who?
11 CLAIRE: You don't know?
12 NAOMI: Know what?
13 CLAIRE: About him and her?
14 NAOMI: You mean they're both ...
15 CLAIRE: Why it's the most talked-about scandal in this
16   church.
17 NAOMI: Has anyone talked to them about this?
18 CLAIRE: Are you kidding? I'm part of the evangelistic
19   committee, not the "mender of pathetic lives" committee.
20   Besides, our goal is to recruit "good people" into the
21   church.
22 NAOMI: Good people like us!
23 CLAIRE: Exactly.
24 NAOMI: Where do we start?
25 CLAIRE: I've got an entire list here of first-rate Christians in
26   other churches — all with excellent participation records
27   and no excess baggage.
28 NAOMI: Great! Let's go then. *(Both exit.)*

Don't Bother Me, Lord, I'm Praying

Theme: Prayer, commitment, listening to God's voice.

Scripture References: Matthew 6:9-13, Matthew 13:14-15, Revelation 3:20

Synopsis: Three individuals get more than they bargained for when they say a "simple" prayer.

Cast: YOUTH 1
YOUTH 2
YOUTH 3
VOICE OF GOD (Off-Stage)

Props: None.

Setting: A youth group retreat. Place three chairs at Center Stage. The setting may be changed to portray men or women at a prayer meeting, National Christian gathering, Bible retreat, or any other occasion where Christians gather together.

1   (*Three YOUTHS are sitting together at Center Stage.*)
2   YOUTH 1: This has been the best youth group retreat I've ever
3   been to.
4   YOUTH 2: You can say that again. Even the Bible studies have
5   been like … interesting!
6   YOUTH 3: Yeah. Are we done with our assignment?
7   YOUTH 1: Yep. All the questions on how God answers
8   prayers. Now let's go to the cafeteria and get something to
9   eat.
10   YOUTH 3: It says here we should close this Bible study with a
11   prayer.
12   YOUTH 1: Oh ... yeah, right. Um … what should we pray?
13   YOUTH 2: (*Folds hands.*) Now I lay me down to sleep, a bag of
14   peanuts at my feet …
15   YOUTH 1: Not that one!
16   YOUTH 3: Besides, I don't like that dying part that comes after
17   it.
18   YOUTH 2: Then what should we do?
19   YOUTH 3: It's gotta be easy. I don't want to think too hard.
20   YOUTH 2: And quick. I'm hungry.
21   YOUTH 1: How about the Lord's Prayer?
22   YOUTH 3: Perfect! You start. (*All fold their hands.*)
23   YOUTH 1: Our Father which art in heaven …
24   VOICE: Yes?
25   YOUTH 1: (*To YOUTH 2*) Did you say something?
26   YOUTH 2: Like what?
27   YOUTH 1: Never mind. (*Returns to praying.*) Our Father which
28   art in heaven …
29   VOICE: Yes?
30   YOUTH 1: (*Turns to YOUTH 3.*) Don't interrupt me while I'm
31   praying.
32   YOUTH 3: I didn't say anything.
33   VOICE: You called me. What's on your mind?
34   YOUTH 1: I didn't call you, I was just saying the Lord's Prayer.
35   I didn't mean anything by it.

1   YOUTH 2: Who's he talking to?

2   YOUTH 3: I don't know.

3   YOUTH 1: Hallowed be thy name.

4   VOICE: Hold it! What did you mean by that?

5   YOUTH 1: By what?

6   VOICE: Hallowed be thy name.

7   YOUTH 1: How am I supposed to know what it means? It's

8   just a part of the prayer.

9   YOUTH 2: *(To YOUTH 3)* He's flipping out.

10   YOUTH 3: *(To YOUTH 1)* If you really want to know, it means

11   sacred, holy, revered ...

12   YOUTH 1: Really? That kind of makes sense. Maybe you should

13   take it now.

14   YOUTH 3: OK. Thy kingdom come. Thy will be done on earth as

15   it is in heaven.

16   VOICE: Do you really mean that?

17   YOUTH 3: Whoa ... who said that?

18   YOUTH 2: Not you too!

19   YOUTH 1: Freaky, isn't it?

20   VOICE: Are you advancing my kingdom by doing my will?

21   YOUTH 3: Well ... I go to church and youth camps.

22   VOICE: That's not what I asked. Are you controlling your temper?

23   Are you setting an example of Christian love and charity, or

24   are you walking the fence and doing your own thing?

25   YOUTH 3: Stop picking on me! I don't have a temper.

26   YOUTH 1: Yes, you do.

27   YOUTH 3: *(To YOUTH 1)* Shut up! Besides, I'm better than some of

28   those other hypocrites at church.

29   VOICE: Pardon me? I thought you were praying for my will to be

30   done, not yours.

31   YOUTH 3: I can't take this kind of pressure!

32   YOUTH 2: Personally, I think you're both cracking up.

33   YOUTH 3: You think you're so smart, you try it!

34   YOUTH 2: OK ... *(Clears his throat.)* Give us this day our daily

35   bread.

1   VOICE: Do you mean that?
2   YOUTH 2: What? *(He looks over and sees the other two grinning.)*
3   VOICE: Do you really trust me to supply you with all your
4   basic needs?
5   YOUTH 2: I — I don't know, man. I'm doing just fine on my
6   own. Besides, I don't really like bread. Now, where was I?
7   Oh, yeah ... Forgive us our debts as we forgive our
8   debtors.
9   VOICE: What about Jason?
10 YOUTH 2: What about that good-for-nothing slime bucket?!
11 VOICE: You *did* ask me to forgive you just as you forgive
12   Jason.
13 YOUTH 2: I can't forgive him. He told lies about me.
14 YOUTH 1: But you did say ...
15 YOUTH 2: I didn't mean it, OK? I can't handle this any longer.
16   *(Puts his hands to his ears.)* I want revenge! I won't listen, I
17   won't! *(YOUTH 2 freezes in this position.)*
18 VOICE: What about you?
19 YOUTH 3: *(Panic response)* What?!
20 VOICE: Will you forgive?
21 YOUTH 3: S-ure. I can do that. I can forgive my sister for
22   ratting me out to my parents.
23 VOICE: Then I can forgive you.
24 YOUTH 3: Whew.
25 VOICE: Now don't you feel renewed?
26 YOUTH 3: Yes I do, Lord. Thanks! Amen!
27 VOICE: Wait a minute. You're not through with the prayer.
28 YOUTH 3: Oh yeah, right. Um ... lead us not into temptation,
29   but deliver us from evil.
30 VOICE: Good. I'll do that. Just don't put yourself in a place
31   where you can be tempted.
32 YOUTH 3: What do you mean by that?
33 VOICE: Quit hanging around with that group that's always
34   getting you into trouble. Change some of your friends.
35 YOUTH 3: But — but —

1   VOICE: Don't be fooled. They like to make you *think* they're
2   having fun, but they're heading straight for destruction.
3   They'll snare you into their plans, and then you'll come
4   crying to me to bail you out.
5   YOUTH 3: I don't understand.
6   VOICE: Sure you do. You've done it lots of times. You get
7   yourself in a bad situation, and then you make all sorts of
8   promises to me if I will only help you out of your
9   mess — promises that you don't intend to keep.
10   YOUTH 3: But they're my friends!
11   VOICE: You want to stay out of temptation? Stay away from
12   them. Can't you see they're leading you down the wrong
13   path?
14   YOUTH 3: No ... no, I can't see! I don't want to see. *(He covers*
15   *his eyes with his hands and freezes in that position.)*
16   VOICE: Well?
17   YOUTH 1: *(Jumps.)* Well what?
18   VOICE: Aren't you going to finish the prayer?
19   YOUTH 1: Uh ... sure. *(Thinks for a second.)* Now I lay me down
20   to sleep, a bag of peanuts at my feet ...
21   VOICE: That's not what you were praying.
22   YOUTH 1: I know, but it's the only safe prayer I can think of.
23   I mean, until now I thought that the Lord's Prayer was just
24   something you said when you couldn't think of anything
25   else to say. I never thought that you actually, you know,
26   listen!
27   VOICE: I listen in more ways than you know. Now go ahead
28   and finish your prayer.
29   YOUTH 1: For thine is the kingdom and the power and the
30   glory forever. Amen. *(Sigh of relief)*
31   VOICE: Do you know what would really bring me glory?
32   YOUTH 1: No, but I have a hunch you're going to tell me.
33   VOICE: Commit your life totally to me.
34   YOUTH 1: Commit my life?!
35   VOICE: Dedicate your whole being to me. Your thought life,

1   your will, your actions. Give it to me, and we can do great
2   things together.
3 YOUTH 1: I can't do that! I want to do my own thing. I can't
4   commit my life to you. I won't say it! *(He covers his mouth*
5   *with his hands and freezes in that position.)*
6 VOICE: *(To audience)* Anyone else want to pray? *(Pause)* It
7   figures. This happens a lot. You can shut me out, but I'll
8   keep speaking; you can close your heart, but I'll keep
9   knocking. You can live your life and pretend I don't exist,
10   but I will always be with you.

Don't Give Up

Theme: Endurance.

**Scripture
Reference:** Hebrews 12:1-3

Synopsis: A climber struggles to keep another motivated when "the journey" seems too much.

Cast: FIRST CLIMBER
SECOND CLIMBER

Costumes: Hiking attire.

Props: A large backpack.

**Director's
Note:** Boulders and high spots can easily be pantomimed. We even used the front pews as a stumbling block to climb over.

Setting: The base of a mountain. You will need several chairs and boxes representing large boulders. They must be large, but sturdy enough to climb over. You will also need an elevated spot or table strong enough for two people to "climb up" to.

1   *(Two CLIMBERS maneuver over several obstacles. The FIRST*
2   *CLIMBER gets over the box with ease. The SECOND CLIMBER*
3   *trips over it. They approach the second obstacle: two folding chairs*
4   *with backs against each other. Again, the FIRST CLIMBER*
5   *climbs over it easily. The SECOND CLIMBER gets over it with*
6   *much difficulty, perhaps even getting stuck in the middle for*
7   *comedic effect. The FIRST CLIMBER sighs and shows signs of*
8   *impatience. They reach the third obstacle: a box or chair on top of*
9   *a large, sturdy table. A chair is next to the table for easier access*
10   *onto the table. The FIRST CLIMBER steps on the chair. He*
11   *reaches a hand out to the SECOND CLIMBER. The SECOND*
12   *CLIMBER reaches the table, panting hard.)*
13   **FIRST CLIMBER: Here, take my hand.**
14   **SECOND CLIMBER:** *(Puffing and panting)* **I ... I can't go any**
15   **farther. You go ahead. Just leave me here.**
16   **FIRST CLIMBER: I'm not going to do that. I'm going to get you**
17   **over this mountain if it's the last thing I do.**
18   **SECOND CLIMBER: It's too hard. I'm not going to make it.**
19   **FIRST CLIMBER: Then get rid of the thing that's holding you**
20   **back.**
21   **SECOND CLIMBER: What's that?**
22   **FIRST CLIMBER: Your backpack. It's weighing you down. Get**
23   **rid of it.**
24   **SECOND CLIMBER: But — but all my** *stuff* **is in there.**
25   **FIRST CLIMBER: What good is it if you can't complete the**
26   **journey?**
27   **SECOND CLIMBER: Oh, all right.** *(Takes off the pack.)*
28   **FIRST CLIMBER: Now doesn't that feel better?**
29   **SECOND CLIMBER: Yeah. I do feel a little lighter.**
30   **FIRST CLIMBER: Great. Let's keep climbing.**
31   **SECOND CLIMBER: I can't breathe. The air is too thin up**
32   **here.**
33   **FIRST CLIMBER:** *(Sighs.)* **Just go slow. Take it one step at a**
34   **time.**
35   **SECOND CLIMBER: It's too big. I can't do it.**

1   FIRST CLIMBER: *(Growing impatient)* **Look. This is *your* mountain.**
2   **Like it or not, you've got to climb it.**
3   SECOND CLIMBER: **But I hate climbing.**
4   FIRST CLIMBER: **But if you don't climb it, you'll never get to the**
5   **top.**
6   SECOND CLIMBER: **What's so great about that?**
7   FIRST CLIMBER: **Well,** *(Pause)* **imagine facing the biggest obstacle**
8   **of your life.**
9   SECOND CLIMBER: **I don't have to imagine it, I'm experiencing**
10   **it!**
11 FIRST CLIMBER: **Now think of sitting on the top of the mountain**
12   **and looking down at what you accomplished to make it up**
13   **here.**
14 SECOND CLIMBER: **Yeah, that would be a great feeling.**
15 FIRST CLIMBER: **And you'll also get a panoramic view of the**
16   **entire valley.**
17 SECOND CLIMBER: **Really?**
18 FIRST CLIMBER: **And then you get to look down and feel proud**
19   **that you made it! Not even a mountain as big as this one is**
20   **going to make you lose faith.**
21 SECOND CLIMBER: **Yeah, proud.**
22 FIRST CLIMBER: *(Extends a hand.)* **So are you with me?**
23 SECOND CLIMBER: **You bet!** *(The SECOND CLIMBER takes the*
24   *hand of the first and allows him to help him onto the table. He then sits*
25   *on the chair and surveys the countryside.)* **Wow. That wasn't so bad**
26   **after all. I knew I could do it once I put my mind to it.** *(Points*
27   *downward.)* **And look at all those people down there. Why,**
28   **they look like little ants!**
29 FIRST CLIMBER: **That's because they *are* ants. You've only**
30   **climbed a few feet. We still have ten thousand feet to go.**
31   *(Points upward. SECOND CLIMBER looks up with mouth gaping*
32   *open.)*
33 SECOND CLIMBER: *(Whining)* **Oh, man! The air is too thin up**
34   **here. I can't make it.**
35 FIRST CLIMBER: *(To audience)* **This is going to be a looong journey.**

47

1   *(Ends with FIRST CLIMBER urging the SECOND CLIMBER ad*
2   *lib: "Let's move," "No, you can't give up," "I wish I'd never prayed for*
3   *patience.")*

Double Agent

Theme: Pride, self-importance.

**Scripture
References:**   John 13:29; John 12:3-5; Psalm 59:12; Proverbs 16:18

Synopsis: Judas pleads his case of self-importance to the people.

Cast: JUDAS
SECRET SERVICE AGENT

Costumes: Dark suit and sunglasses for Secret Service Agent. Biblical robe for Judas.

Props: Billfold.

Setting: Old Testament era meets twenty-first century security.

1   (*A SECRET SERVICE AGENT stands stoically Stage Right.*
2   *JUDAS enters from back behind the audience and converses with*
3   *several audience members, calling them by name.*)
4   **JUDAS: I don't believe it! He puts me in charge of the treasury,**
5   **and then he doesn't listen to me!** (*Turns to audience member.*)
6   **I** *told* **him the oil was best used if we sell it and give it to**
7   **the poor. I** *told* **him it was a waste to have that — that**
8   ***woman*** (*Said with disgust*) **pour it all over his feet.** (*Turns to*
9   *another audience member.*) **Not only that, she dried his feet**
10   **with her hair! How disgusting!** (*Addresses entire audience*
11   *after making his way to the front.*) **You know who I am, don't**
12   **you? I'm Judas. You know, Jesus' most** *trusted* **disciple. No**
13   **one else controls and distributes the money given to Jesus**
14   **except me.** (*Pause*) **Well, you certainly wouldn't trust a**
15   **bunch of uneducated fishermen to add and subtract**
16   **correctly, would you?** (*Pauses and looks around.*) **Yeah, I**
17   **know Matthew is educated too, but he's a tax collector!**
18   **Have you forgotten how badly they cheat and pocket your**
19   **money for their own? So you can see how I'm really**
20   **important to Jesus. More important than** *Peter*. (*Again said*
21   *with disgust.*) **And I'm definitely more important than**
22   **John. That kid clings onto his every word!** (*AGENT*
23   *approaches.*) **And then there's —**
24   **AGENT: You're Judas Iscariot, aren't you?**
25   **JUDAS:** (*Startled*) **Who are you?**
26   **AGENT:** (*Takes out his billfold and quickly opens and closes it before*
27   *JUDAS can see what's inside.*) **I'm a member of the S.S.S.**
28   **JUDAS: The S.S.S.?**
29   **AGENT: Sanhedrin Secret Service. We've been monitoring**
30   **your activities for some time now.**
31   **JUDAS: I knew it! I** *told* **Jesus to stop performing miracles on**
32   **the Sabbath. I** *told* **him it was only going to make the**
33   **Pharisees angry. I** *told* **him —**
34   **AGENT: We're not monitoring Jesus' activities. We already**
35   **know what he does. We've been monitoring** *you*.

1 JUDAS: Say what?

2 AGENT: You're one of Jesus' disciples.

3 JUDAS: His most *trusted* disciple, yes.

4 AGENT: You're also not happy with the way he runs things.

5 JUDAS: Well ... I thought we'd have an army by now. I thought
6 we'd be fighting the Roman Empire. I really thought I
7 was in the midst of something special. But all Jesus talks
8 about is peace and heaven.

9 AGENT: The Sanhedrin wants to speak with him. We need
10 someone to inform us of his whereabouts.

11 JUDAS: I'm no stooge.

12 AGENT: Caiaphas only wants to talk with him. Possibly give
13 him a warning concerning his questionable activities.

14 JUDAS: Talking doesn't sound too bad. Is that all they want to
15 do?

16 AGENT: Maybe give him a slap on the wrist and tell him to
17 behave himself. The point is, if he continues to anger the
18 high officials, they'll go after him. If they do that, they'll
19 go after all his disciples. Are you willing to take the fall
20 with him?

21 JUDAS: I'm not the one healing on the Sabbath!

22 AGENT: Doesn't matter. It's guilt by association.

23 JUDAS: I could lose everything!

24 AGENT: Look, just come down to the Sanhedrin tonight.
25 Caiaphas will just ask you a few questions. If you look
26 like you're willing to cooperate by providing ... you
27 know — just a few details on his whereabouts, I'm sure
28 you'll be looked on with favor. Possibly even given a cash
29 reward.

30 JUDAS: I could always use a little money.

31 AGENT: Let's go then. *(They start to exit.)*

32 JUDAS: It's amazing you know so much about me.

33 AGENT: It's the glasses. It helps us blend in with the crowd
34 without getting noticed.

Evangelistic Task Force

Theme: Judging others, evangelism, discipleship.

Scripture Reference: Matthew 9:9-13

Synopsis: Two individuals make it their mission to help Jesus recruit followers, only to become frustrated at Jesus' "wrong choices."

Cast: RECRUITMENT OFFICER
AIDE

Props: A stack of papers.

Setting: The time of Christ — Jerusalem.

1 *(The RECRUITMENT OFFICER paces back and forth across the*
2 *stage. Throughout the sketch, the AIDE frantically tries to keep*
3 *up with the OFFICER, picking up the papers he throws on the*
4 *floor while answering his questions.)*
5 **RECRUITMENT OFFICER: Aide! Where in blazes is my aide?**
6 **He should have been here by now.**
7 **AIDE:** *(Runs up, stumbles, and is obviously nervous.)* **Here I am, sir.**
8 *(Hands the RECRUITMENT OFFICER a stack of papers.)*
9 **RECRUITMENT OFFICER: It's about time. I ordered these**
10 **hours ago.**
11 **AIDE: I know, sir, but ...**
12 **RECRUITMENT OFFICER: Did you know that Jesus is out**
13 **there right now, recruiting his twelve disciples on his**
14 **own?**
15 **AIDE: No, sir ...**
16 **RECRUITMENT OFFICER: It's terrible! He's making all the**
17 **wrong choices, hanging out with the wrong crowds. Our**
18 **mission is to set him straight!** *(Looks at papers.)* **Now, what**
19 **do we have?**
20 **AIDE: Caiaphas the high priest would be a good candidate.**
21 **RECRUITMENT OFFICER: Yes, yes, but too busy with the**
22 **Sanhedrin.** *(Flings paper onto the floor, which is immediately*
23 *retrieved by the AIDE.)*
24 **AIDE: Nicodemus is a good choice.**
25 **RECRUITMENT OFFICER: Too much sneaking around at**
26 **night. If he wants to know about Jesus, let him come**
27 **forward in the daylight.** *(Tosses paper on floor. AIDE retrieves*
28 *it.)*
29 **AIDE: Herod? He would be a great choice to convert the**
30 **masses.**
31 **RECRUITMENT OFFICER:** *(Stops his pacing for a moment and*
32 *thinks.)* **True. Herod would be an excellent candidate.**
33 *(Shakes his head.)* **But that adultery thing with his sister-in-**
34 **law spoils that idea. If John the Baptist didn't approve,**
35 **neither would Jesus.** *(Tosses paper.)* **Man, I wish he**

1   wouldn't be so picky! What's our count up to?

2   AIDE: *(Quickly shuffles his papers and hands one to him.)* Um ...

3   seven fishermen so far.

4   RECRUITMENT OFFICER: *(Shocked)* Fishermen! Has he gone

5   mad? They're not appropriate at all!

6   AIDE: They seemed like a sincere lot.

7   RECRUITMENT OFFICER: Sincere but smelly, uneducated,

8   and rough around the edges. They'll offend people, mark

9   my words. *(Crushes paper and throws to the ground. Again the*

10   *AIDE picks up after him.)*

11   AIDE: They say he's recruiting more educated men. Today he

12   was seen talking with Matthew.

13   RECRUITMENT OFFICER: The tax collector! He's the worst

14   sinner yet! Why, Jesus might as well hang out with harlots

15   and criminals!

16   AIDE: *(Hands another paper.)* He's scheduled to eat dinner with

17   them tonight at Matthew's house.

18   RECRUITMENT OFFICER: What? What is he thinking?

19   AIDE: He says the sinners are the ones who need him the most.

20   RECRUITMENT OFFICER: *(Tosses the paper.)* We've got to nip

21   this in the bud before he starts to recruit even more

22   delinquent lowlife. I mean, it's fine *if* they actually turn

23   their lives around, but they're not suited for the work

24   that's required of being a disciple.

25   AIDE: There is one disciple that seems to have all the

26   prerequisites you specified. He's educated, smart, and

27   very zealous for his people's cause.

28   RECRUITMENT OFFICER: Who is that?

29   AIDE: *(Hands him a paper.)* Judas Iscariot.

30   RECRUITMENT OFFICER: Ah, now there's a man who'll

31   make a difference. We just need to encourage Jesus to pick

32   more men like him and less like this Matthew person.

33   AIDE: I have an entire list of religious leaders, holy

34   theologians, and qualified perfect people that might be

35   just who Jesus needs.

1   RECRUITMENT OFFICER: *(Takes the list.)* Excellent. We'll give
2   this to Jesus first thing in the morning. I'm sure he'll
3   realize the importance of calling only the most
4   outstanding individuals to his service. Now ... what
5   grand dialog is he using to entice his people to follow?
6   AIDE: He simply says, "Follow me."
7   RECRUITMENT OFFICER: *(Hangs and shakes his head.)* We've
8   got to work on his recruitment speech. *(They exit.)*

Fallen Hero

Theme: Pre-Easter, self-importance.

Scripture References: Matthew 26:3, Luke 3:2, John 18:14

Synopsis: Caiaphas is shocked and offended to learn that someone is gaining more notoriety than he has.

Cast: CAIAPHAS
1ST WOMAN
2ND WOMAN
3RD WOMAN

Costumes: Biblical clothing. A simple head covering works well for the women. A regal tunic will do for Caiaphas.

Props: None.

Setting: New Testament times.

1　*(Three WOMEN run up to the stage. All enter from different*
2　*locations and meet mid-center.)*
3　**1ST WOMAN: Have you seen him?**
4　**2ND WOMAN: No. Have you?** *(CAIAPHAS enters Stage Left.*
5　*The WOMEN see him.)*
6　**3RD WOMAN: Girls, it's him — It's —** *(Said with adoration)*
7　**it's — Caiaphas!** *(The WOMEN run to him. He is used to this*
8　*kind of adoration.)*
9　**CAIAPHAS: Hello, ladies.** *(The WOMEN giggle as they wrap their*
10　*arms around his.)*
11　**1ST WOMAN: Caiaphas, you are *soooo* wonderful!**
12　**CAIAPHAS: I know.**
13　**2ND WOMAN: No one in the Sanhedrin is as smart as you.**
14　**CAIAPHAS: That's true.**
15　**3RD WOMAN: We all look to you as a great leader.**
16　**CAIAPHAS: Naturally.**
17　**1ST WOMAN: You're also the best teacher of the Scriptures.**
18　**CAIAPHAS: Of course.**
19　**2ND WOMAN: Second to Jesus.**
20　**CAIAPHAS: Excuse me?**
21　**3RD WOMAN: Have you heard Jesus preach yet?**
22　**CAIAPHAS:** *(Confused)* **What?**
23　**1ST WOMAN: Wasn't it amazing how he fed all those people**
24　**with just two fish and five loaves of bread?**
25　**2ND WOMAN: I was there! They even had leftovers.**
26　**3RD WOMAN: No! Really?**
27　**CAIAPHAS: Um ... ladies? I think we're losing our focus here.**
28　*(Points at himself.)*
29　**1ST WOMAN: Did you see him heal those lepers?**
30　**2ND WOMAN: What about the man with the shriveled hand?**
31　**He healed him last Saturday.**
32　**CAIAPHAS: On the Sabbath?**
33　**3RD WOMAN: Isn't he wonderful?**
34　**1ST WOMAN: Let's go find him!** *(They all enthusiastically agree.*
35　*CAIAPHAS is stunned.)*

1   **2ND WOMAN: I heard he's down by the Red Sea.**

2   **3RD WOMAN: Let's go!** *(The WOMEN exit together, leaving*

3   *CAIAPHAS to stand alone Center Stage. He tries to contemplate*

4   *what just happened. This is crucial. The longer he stands there*

5   *and uses body language and hand gestures to sort through the*

6   *recent scenario, the funnier it will be.)*

7   **CAIAPHAS: I — I think this Jesus person just stole my**

8   **thunder! That doesn't happen to me!** *(Lower lip quivers.)*

9   **The Sanhedrin is going to hear about this. Dad!**

10   *(CAIAPHAS exits.)*

For the Love of Hate

Theme: Discipleship, love.

Scripture Reference: Luke 14:25-33 (NKJV)

Synopsis: Two teenagers finally have justification to hate their families — and they're waaaay too excited about it.

Cast: DOUG
MICHELLE
JORDAN
(Gender and names may be changed)

Props: Bible.

Setting: Outside a church building.

1	*(DOUG is standing Center Stage. MICHELLE enters.)*
2	MICHELLE: *(Excited)* **Hey Doug, did you hear the pastor's**
3	**sermon on Luke 14?**
4	DOUG: **Yeah, wasn't it great?**
5	MICHELLE: **I haven't been this excited since my acne cleared**
6	**up!**
7	DOUG: **Me too! This will finally unite all the teenagers of the**
8	**world!**
9	MICHELLE: **So what do you think of your dad?**
10	DOUG: **I hate him.** *(Smiles.)* **Isn't it great?**
11	MICHELLE: **And I hate my mom!**
12	DOUG: **What about your brother and sister?**
13	MICHELLE: **I *loathe* them!**
14	DOUG: **That's a good word.**
15	MICHELLE: **Thank you.**
16	DOUG: **How about "despise"? I despise my sister.**
17	MICHELLE: **I abhor my brother.**
18	DOUG: **I detest my entire family!**
19	MICHELLE: **And I am repulsed by my family.**
20	DOUG: **Ooooh, that sounds really calloused!**
21	MICHELLE: **Is that a good thing?**
22	DOUG: **Who cares? This sure is fun!** *(JORDAN enters.)*
23	JORDAN: **Hi, guys. What are you doing?**
24	MICHELLE: **Practicing our hate.**
25	JORDAN: **Practicing your what?**
26	DOUG: **Our hate! We have scriptural permission to hate our**
27	**families.**
28	JORDAN: **How do you figure that?**
29	MICHELLE: *(Opens Bible.)* **It says in Luke 14:26, "If anyone**
30	**comes to me and does not hate his father, mother, wife and**
31	**children, brothers and sisters ... he cannot be my**
32	**disciple."**
33	DOUG: **We teenagers can finally be justified in our logic.**
34	JORDAN: **Our logic?**
35	DOUG: **You know, the ability to logically deduce everything to**

1   its wrong conclusion!
2   MICHELLE: And we're good at that, too.
3   DOUG: You bet.
4   JORDAN: You're better than you think.
5   MICHELLE: What do you mean?
6   JORDAN: Well, if you would have listened to the rest of the
7   sermon, the pastor went on to say that our love for Jesus
8   must be so great that the love we feel for our families and
9   even ourselves would seem like hate.
10   DOUG: So what are you saying?
11   JORDAN: So, I'm afraid you're still going to have to love your
12   families.
13   MICHELLE: But that's not fair!
14   DOUG: *(Angry)* What are you going to do next? Cancel
15   Christmas?
16   JORDAN: Sorry, guys, but following Jesus is not easy. We have
17   to be willing to give up all that we have.
18   MICHELLE: My makeup! Don't tell me I have to give up my
19   mascara.
20   JORDAN: *(Taken aback)* Uh ... I think you can keep that for
21   now.
22   MICHELLE: Whew. That was a close one.
23   DOUG: I'm going home.
24   MICHELLE: Don't you want to hang out at the mall?
25   DOUG: Nah. I need to get the snake out of my sister's bed.

The Giant Roars

Theme: Fear, trust in God, facing challenges.

Scripture Reference: 1 Samuel 17

Synopsis: The Israelites are afraid. They see Goliath as a barrier to the battle, but David sees him from a different perspective.

Cast: DAVID
GOLIATH
CAPTAIN
SHAMMAH
ELIAB
SOLDIER
SIX TO EIGHT SOLDIERS (optional)

Costumes: Old Testament costumes — optional.

Props: None (David's slingshot is pantomimed).

Setting: A place called Sochoh, where the Israelites are facing off against the Philistines in battle.

1   *(The scene begins with six to eight SOLDIERS standing in two*
2   *rows. The CAPTAIN paces in front of his men. He stops short*
3   *when he hears the voice of GOLIATH. The SOLDIERS' faces*
4   *turn from sober to fearful as they look over the audience's heads to*
5   *the "supposed giant.")*
6   VOICE: *(From Off-stage)* **You're nothing but a bunch of yellow-**
7   **belly cowards. Is there no one brave enough to fight me?**
8   CAPTAIN: **Just ignore him, men.**
9   SHAMMAH: **How do you ignore someone who's ten feet tall?!**
10   VOICE: **You're a pathetic bunch of worms! How simple can it**
11   **be? Choose your best man to fight me. If he kills me,**
12   **which I doubt, our army will gladly lay down our swords**
13   **and become your servants.**
14   SHAMMAH: **Yeah, like we're dumb enough to take** *that*
15   **challenge.**
16   VOICE: **You say your God is so powerful. Ha! I defy your God.**
17   **You men should crawl back under the rock where you**
18   **came from!**
19   CAPTAIN: **Men, are we going to let him talk to us like this?**
20   SOLDIER: **There's no shame in being a worm.**
21   CAPTAIN: **Who will protect our honor and fight Goliath?**
22   SHAMMAH: **How about you, Captain?**
23   CAPTAIN: **This is no time to be insolent! I need our strongest**
24   **and most experienced warrior to fight this giant. Now ...**
25   **who will it be?**
26   DAVID: *(Hidden behind the other SOLDIERS)* **I'll do it!**
27   CAPTAIN: **Who said that?**
28   DAVID: *(Raises his hand and jumps up and down.)* **Me! Me! I'll do**
29   **it!** *(ELIAB looks in the back line, then turns to the CAPTAIN.)*
30   ELIAB: **Will you give me a minute, Captain?** *(ELIAB goes behind*
31   *the line and pulls DAVID out on the other side.)* **What do you**
32   **think you're doing?**
33   DAVID: **What! What did I do?**
34   ELIAB: **How dare you show up here! Who's taking care of the**
35   **sheep?**

1   DAVID: The sheep are fine. Father sent me here to bring food.
2   ELIAB: Don't give me that. You came to see the battle.
3   DAVID: Doesn't look like much of a battle to me. Why won't
4   you fight this bully? *(ELIAB takes DAVID by the collar and*
5   *points out toward the audience.)*
6   ELIAB: Do you see that man? He's ten feet tall. Look how he's
7   covered from head to toe in armor.
8   SHAMMAH: *(Steps up.)* His sword alone will take you out with
9   one swipe.
10   DAVID: OK. He's a really *big* bully.
11   ELIAB: Are you so ignorant that you can't see that he's too big
12   to fight?
13   DAVID: Too big to fight? He's too big to miss!
14   SOLDIER: *(To CAPTAIN)* Captain! We've got a sucker — I
15   mean, a soldier — willing to take on the giant.
16   CAPTAIN: Really? Who's that?
17   SOLDIER: *(Points.)* Eliab's little brother.
18   CAPTAIN: *(Walks over and examines DAVID. He looks in disbelief.)*
19   You're kidding me. He's just a boy!
20   DAVID: I can do it, sir! *(ELIAB tries to put his hand over DAVID's*
21   *mouth, but DAVID pushes it away.)* I've killed lions and
22   bears with nothing but my slingshot. I can take on this
23   Philistine slug!
24   CAPTAIN: Very well, then. *(Turns to the SOLDIER.)* Lieutenant,
25   fetch a suit of armor for the boy.
26   DAVID: I'm not used to wearing any armor, sir. All I need is
27   my slingshot and a few rocks.
28   SHAMMAH: The only rocks he's got are in his head.
29   ELIAB: Don't listen to him, Captain. He's always been full of
30   grand ideas. He's not quite right upstairs. *(Points to his*
31   *temple.)*
32   CAPTAIN: Your brother's got a point …
33   DAVID: Just because you're all too *chicken* to fight him,
34   doesn't mean I am!
35   CAPTAIN: *(Stiffens)* Prepare him for battle. *(DAVID pantomimes*

1   *preparing his slingshot. SHAMMAH turns to DAVID.)*
2 **SHAMMAH: David, don't do this. What are we going to tell**
3   **Father when you're dead?**
4 **DAVID: Tell him that this is the day the Lord will deliver**
5   **Goliath into *my* hands. No longer will the Philistines**
6   **defy the army of the living God.** *(DAVID starts to wind up*
7   *his slingshot and exits. All the SOLDIERS smile and wave,*
8   *including ELIAB and SHAMMAH.)*
9 **SOLDIER: Good luck, David!**
10 **ELIAB: Have fun fighting the giant.**
11 **SHAMMAH:** *(To ELIAB)* **Do you think he has a chance?**
12 **ELIAB: It'll take a miracle.**
13 **ELIAB and SHAMMAH:** *(Together)* **Bye-bye!**
14
15   *(Director's Note: This sketch was created with the intention of an*
16   *"open ending." The ending was then told during the sermon.*
17   *However, for those who want a more complete ending, see the next*
18   *sketch entitled "The Giant Surprise.")*

The Giant Surprise

Theme: Overconfidence, self-importance.

**Scripture
Reference:** 1 Samuel 17

Synopsis: A giant's overconfidence becomes his downfall.

Cast: DAVID
GOLIATH

Costumes: Old Testament costumes and armor for Goliath (optional).

Props: A sword for Goliath. David's slingshot is pantomimed.

Setting: A place called Sochoh, the battlefield of the Philistines verses the Israelites.

1   (*GOLIATH enters and addresses the audience.*)

2   GOLIATH: Cowards! Every one of you spineless worms! You

3   think your God is so great? *Ha!* Is he greater than me? I

4   think not. I'm the strongest, the wisest, and let us not

5   forget, the best-looking of all the warriors. You say your

6   God can create life? I've got news for you. I can create

7   death! Come on down, and I'll slice your heads off and

8   show you how it's done. (*DAVID enters and walks up to*

9   *GOLIATH and tugs at his outfit. GOLIATH tries to brush him*

10   *away while still addressing the audience.*) Of course once

11   you're dead, you won't be able to utilize what you

12   learned, so that could be a drawback.

13   DAVID: (*Continuing to tug or poke at GOLIATH's clothing*) Excuse

14   me, Mr. Goliath.

15   GOLIATH: Go away, kid. (*Back to the audience*) Now what was I

16   saying? Oh, yeah. Isn't anybody man enough to fight me?

17   You are lower than the creatures that crawl on their

18   bellies! (*DAVID continues to poke at GOLIATH's clothing.*

19   *GOLIATH is distracted.*) I said, "Go away." You're

20   bothering me.

21   DAVID: I'm man enough.

22   GOLIATH: Why did you even bother to show up for battle? I

23   *defy* the army of Israel. (*Tries to wave off DAVID.*) Beat it,

24   kid.

25   DAVID: You don't scare me.

26   GOLIATH: (*Continues to ignore DAVID.*) I'll tell you what — I'll

27   make it easy for you. Choose one person to fight me.

28   Loser serves the winner.

29   DAVID: The choice has been made. *I'm* going to fight you.

30   GOLIATH: (*Turns his attention to DAVID.*) You? (*Scans him up*

31   *and down.*) You're the *best* they can do? (*Turns to audience.*)

32   Come on, people, give me a challenge! (*DAVID begins to*

33   *wind up his slingshot.*) The kid doesn't even have any

34   armor! You're not only cowards, you're stupid! I curse

35   your God and your silly little army. I'm going to kill

1   "Tiny" here and let his body rot where it drops. I'm going
2   to — (DAVID *shoots the stone from his slingshot and GOLIATH*
3   *falls to the ground.*)
4 DAVID: Never call a man with a slingshot "Tiny." (*Exits.*)

Got Christ?

Theme: Living water, eternal life.

Scripture References: John 4:14; 7:37-39; Revelation 21:6; 22:17

Synopsis: Two people find what they're looking for when they drink from the "living water" in this commercial about that "other" drink.

Cast: (Male/female roles interchangeable)
SALESPERSON
BRANDON
DANIEL

Props: Pitcher (optional) and several glasses of water.

Setting: A commercial set. You will need a table to hold the pitcher and glasses.

1   *(A SALESPERSON stands next to a table with a pitcher and*
2   *several glasses of water. BRANDON and DANIEL enter.)*
3   DANIEL: Man, that was the driest journey we've ever been on.
4   BRANDON: I'm really thirsty.
5   DANIEL: How could you still be thirsty when you drank up all
6   our water?
7   BRANDON: I couldn't help it. It didn't satisfy me.
8   DANIEL: Yeah, but now we're left with nothing.
9   *(SALESPERSON approaches.)*
10   SALESPERSON: Excuse me. Have you ... *(Pauses for effect as he*
11   *holds up the glass)* got Christ?
12   BRANDON: What?
13   SALESPERSON: The hope of our salvation. One drink from
14   the living water, and your thirst will be quenched forever.
15   DANIEL: Trust me, his thirst is *never* satisfied. *(BRANDON*
16   *takes the glass and takes a sip.)*
17   BRANDON: Wow, he's right!
18   DANIEL: No way.
19   BRANDON: I'm serious. For the first time in my life, I don't
20   feel thirsty.
21   SALESPERSON: It's true. When you drink from the spring of
22   life, the water continually replenishes itself within you.
23   *(Turns toward DANIEL.)* What about you? Have you ...
24   *(Holds up a glass)* got Christ?
25   DANIEL: I don't need any of that. I'm rarely thirsty. Besides,
26   I'm on a quest of my own.
27   SALESPERSON: So have you ever found what you're looking
28   for?
29   DANIEL: Well ... no. But if I follow enough roads, I'm sure to
30   find the one that's right for me.
31   SALESPERSON: How about a drink from the spring of eternal
32   life? One sip and you'll no longer need to take any more
33   side trips. You'll discover that the only way to truth and
34   life is through Jesus.
35   DANIEL: *(Shrugs and takes the glass.)* Well, I've tried everything

1   **else. What can it hurt?** *(Takes a drink. Looks at the glass with*
2   *surprise.)* **Wow! Why have I been searching all these years**
3   **when the answer was here all along?**
4   **BRANDON: Isn't it great?!**
5   **DANIEL: How much do I owe you for this water?**
6   **SALESPERSON: It's free to all who search for truth.**
7   **DANIEL: Come on, let's go tell all our friends about this.** *(As*
8   *DANIEL and BRANDON exit, the SALESPERSON calls after*
9   *them.)*
10   **SALESPERSON: Don't forget to consume plenty of milk and**
11   **meat at a good Bible-based church.** *(Turns and addresses the*
12   *audience.)* **Scripture says that whoever believes in Jesus,**
13   **rivers of living water will flow out of their heart. So with**
14   **that in mind, have you ...** *(Holds up glass)* **got Christ?**
15   *(Freezes for a second, then exits.)*

Great One Tells Great Tales

Theme: Pre-Easter, worldliness.

**Scripture
References:** Luke 3:1; 9:7-9; 23:7-8; Mark 6:17-19.

Synopsis: A lighthearted look at Herod as he agrees to answer
questions regarding his reign in Galilee.

Cast: HEROD
ANNOUNCER

Costumes: New Testament-style robes if available, with a king's
crown for Herod.

Props: Herod may hold a bottle of wine in one hand and a
turkey leg for a scepter in the other (optional).

Setting: New Testament times.

1   *(ANNOUNCER stands behind the podium.)*
2   ANNOUNCER: Good evening, ladies and gentlemen. We have
3   a real treat for you today. Herod is right here in Jerusalem,
4   and he has kindly agreed to address the audience and
5   answer questions regarding his role as King. May I
6   present Herod Antipas! *(ANNOUNCER claps as HEROD*
7   *enters holding a turkey leg/scepter in one hand and a bottle of*
8   *wine in the other. HEROD raises his arms toward the audience.)*
9   HEROD: Thank you, thank you one and all. Please don't clap.
10   *(Clapping dies down. Suddenly motions to himself.)* OK ... clap.
11   *(People start again. HEROD turns to ANNOUNCER.)* What
12   can I say? They love me.
13   ANNOUNCER: Now, Herod ... *(Pauses for a second)* um ... may I
14   call you Herod?
15   HEROD: Actually, I prefer to be called "The Great One."
16   ANNOUNCER: OK ... *(Struggles with words)* Great One. Tell
17   me, how did you become King of Judea?
18   HEROD: It's quite simple, really. I was appointed by the
19   Roman senate. What a bunch of great guys. Worth every
20   bit we paid them.
21   ANNOUNCER: One of the biggest controversies about you, as
22   you already know, is the fact that you married your
23   brother's wife. How were you able to get away with that?
24   HEROD: Hey, I'm the King! Need I say more?
25   ANNOUNCER: What does your brother say about you
26   stealing Herodias?
27   HEROD: Stealing is such a *strong* word. I prefer "pocketing
28   what should have been mine."
29   ANNOUNCER: Didn't John the Baptist condemn your actions
30   and publicly announce that you were both in the wrong?
31   HEROD: Now, now. Like the Baptist, we don't want to lose our
32   heads over this. *(Playfully jabs ANNOUNCER in the ribs.)*
33   Get it ... huh? That reminds me of a joke. What do John
34   the Baptist and the horseman of Sleepy Hollow have in
35   common? *(ANNOUNCER looks confused.)* They're both

1   **headless! Get it?** *(HEROD slaps his knee and laughs at his own*
2   *joke. ANNOUNCER still looks confused.)* **I got another one.**
3   **Why was John the Baptist the last to finish the race?**
4   *(Pause)* **He couldn't get a-head!** *(Again, he laughs at his own*
5   *joke. ANNOUNCER pretends to laugh. HEROD wipes his eyes.)*
6   **I just crack myself up.**
7 ANNOUNCER: **What is your opinion about the rumors that**
8   **Jesus of Nazareth is actually John the Baptist returning**
9   **from the dead?**
10 HEROD: **Oh, that would be cool to see. I heard he's doing**
11   **miracles like healing people, raising them from the dead,**
12   **walking on water ... yes, I'd definitely like to meet him**
13   **someday.**
14 ANNOUNCER: **You're going to have your chance. The**
15   **religious leaders have captured him, and Pilate is sending**
16   **him here to be questioned by** *you.*
17 HEROD: **Really? Then let's go meet them in the main court.**
18   *(HEROD and the ANNOUNCER start to exit.)* **This is going**
19   **to be good. I wonder if he'll perform a miracle for me or**
20   **something.** *(Pause)* **Do you think he'll like my Sleepy**
21   **Hollow joke?**
22 ANNOUNCER: **No one likes that joke.** *(Both exit.)*

Guardianship 101

Theme: Listening, spiritual guidance.

Scripture References: Psalm 91:11-12; 34:7

Synopsis: The Angel instructor teaches the various methods of communicating with humans, sometimes resorting to drastic measures.

Cast: ANGEL
MALE
FEMALE

Costumes: Angel outfit if available. A choir robe usually works well. Apron for Female.

Props: A remote for Male, a pointing stick, a megaphone, a Nerf bat, or a pillow.

Setting: First heaven and then a home, for which you'll need either a couch or several chairs pushed together.

1   *(ANGEL stands Center Stage, pointing stick in hand. She*
2   *addresses the class as though the adults have a childlike*
3   *understanding. The students are definitely beginners. The MALE*
4   *and FEMALE stand motionless to the right.)*
5   **ANGEL: Welcome, fellow angels, to the class "Guardianship**
6   **one-oh-one." For all of you who will continue on and**
7   **actually become guardian angels, it's essential to learn the**
8   **basic method of communication with your charges.** *(Walks*
9   *over to the MALE and FEMALE and points at them with her*
10   *stick.)* **Notice we have two individuals of the *human***
11   ***persuasion*. Both have a head, two eyes, nose, mouth,**
12   **trunk and limbs. Notice how each also has two ears. This**
13   **device is used for listening, although we're going to find**
14   **that the ear is a much more complicated body part than**
15   **the rest. You see, in the spiritual world, the ears are**
16   **directly connected to the mind and the heart.** *(Continues to*
17   *point using her stick.)* **The mind not focused on God will be**
18   **completely shut down from our suggestions.** *(Points to*
19   *heart.)* **A heart not in tune with God is nearly impossible**
20   **to penetrate. A heart totally shut down requires prayer to**
21   **jump-start it back to the spiritual world. However, that's**
22   **something you'll learn in your graduate class. For now,**
23   *(Waves the pointing stick at the MALE and FEMALE)* **let's**
24   **release them back into their own little existence, and I'll**
25   **demonstrate the various methods we use to communicate**
26   **with them.** *(MAN sits down on a couch/chair, picks up a remote,*
27   *points it at the television/audience, and rapidly clicks away at the*
28   *channels. Mouth is open and he has a trance-like look about him.*
29   *The FEMALE goes in the opposite direction and starts to wash*
30   *dishes. This may be pantomimed.)* **Now, when a heart is in**
31   **tune with God, we only need to deliver a breath of a**
32   **suggestion. These are known as "God whispers."** *(Goes*
33   *over to the WOMAN and speaks in her direction.)* **The children**
34   **are way too quiet.**
35   **FEMALE:** *(Stops what she's doing and looks around.)* **You know, the**

1   children are unusually quiet.
2   ANGEL: They said they were going to play in the garage.
3   Maybe you should check on them.
4   FEMALE: I think I'd better make sure they're OK. *(Wipes her*
5   *hands and exits.)*
6   ANGEL: *(To audience)* You see how with just a *whisper* of a
7   suggestion she responds to our promptings, and a
8   potentially dangerous situation is avoided. Now let's
9   rewind that. *(Waves the pointing stick. The FEMALE re-enters,*
10   *but she is walking backwards as though she is a video on rewind.*
11   *She resumes washing the dishes.)* Let's assume it is with this
12   individual that we need to communicate. *(Crosses to*
13   *MALE.)* This one is a much tougher egg to crack. He's
14   been so engrossed with his job and extracurricular
15   activities that he no longer listens to the whispers. *(Talks*
16   *to the MALE.)* The children are way too quiet. *(No response.*
17   *ANGEL speaks a little louder.)* You'd better go check on
18   them. *(No response. MALE continues to click away at the*
19   *remote.)* I said to *check on the kids!* *(Still no response. ANGEL*
20   *turns to audience.)* Obviously, he needs a little more
21   prompting. It is wise at this time to add a smidgeon of
22   volume. *(Pulls out a megaphone from behind the chair.)* Yo!
23   *Your kids are up to no good — check them out!* *(MALE*
24   *blinks, looks around, and turns to FEMALE.)*
25   MALE: Hey, honey, where are the kids?
26   FEMALE: I think they're out in the garage.
27   MALE: Oh. OK. *(He resumes rapidly clicking the remote control.)*
28   ANGEL: Clearly we've made some progress here. However,
29   he's still stuck in his own little world and isn't in tune
30   with God's promptings. Now is the time for more
31   desperate measures. *(Pulls out a Nerf bat or a pillow and beats*
32   *him across the head, then uses the megaphone.)* Your kids are
33   *playing with your power tools again!* *(MALE's eyes pop*
34   *open. He turns to FEMALE.)*
35   MALE: Did you say they're in the garage?

1 FEMALE: Yes.
2 MALE: *(Stands.)* I hope they're not getting into my stuff. *(He*
3   *exits, then is heard Off-stage.)* **Hey! Get away from that chain**
4   **saw! Rebekah, drop that staple gun!** *(Re-enters and sits on the*
5   *couch.)* **Can you believe those kids? They were going to**
6   **play war using my power tools!**
7 FEMALE: **It was a good thing you went out to check. God must**
8   **have been speaking to you.**
9 MALE: **That had nothing to do with it. It takes common sense**
10   **and the ability to be alert to your surroundings. Face it,**
11   **hon. You just don't have the instincts that I have.** *(He picks*
12   *up the remote and resumes clicking away with a deadpan*
13   *expression on his face.)*
14 ANGEL: **An important final note, students, is that we angels**
15   **rarely** *(Looks at MALE with disgust)* **get any credit for our**
16   **effort.** *(Picks up the Nerf bat and hits him over the head again,*
17   *then exits in a huff.)*
18 MALE: *(Blinks, then turns to FEMALE.)* **Did you say something?**

Heaven's Hotline

Theme: Prayers, listening.

Scripture References: John 9:31; John 14:13-14; 1 John 5:14-15

Synopsis: An individual tries to make a prayer request via telephone, only to find frustration at the voice mail system instead.

Cast: ACTOR
VOICE/SATAN

Costumes: Satan costume. Cape and/or horns work well. Satan also needs to wear a telephone headset.

Props: Phone.

Sound Effect: Beeps (two different tones).

Setting: A call center. You will need a table with a sign at each end. One says, "Heaven's Hotline." The other says, "Direct Prayers to God at This Phone."

1   *(A telephone sits centered on a table. There is a sign at each end.*
2   *The first one reads, "Heaven's Hotline." The second one says,*
3   *"Direct Prayers to God at This Phone." ACTOR enters, looks at*
4   *the signs, and decides to pick up the receiver.)*
5   **VOICE:** *(From Off-stage)* **Hello. You have reached Heaven's**
6   **Hotline, enabling you to speak to the Almighty himself.**
7   **Press one for English, two for Spanish, and three for**
8   **tongues.** *(The ACTOR presses a button. A beep is heard.)* **If this**
9   **is a standard prayer, press one. If this is a request for**
10   **something you want, press two. If this is an emergency,**
11   **press three.** *(The ACTOR presses a button. Beep.)* **You have**
12   **chosen Emergency Prayer Hotline. If this is an actual life**
13   **or death emergency, press one. If this is a perceived**
14   **emergency on your part and no one else seems to care,**
15   **press two. If you have reached this recording in error, or**
16   **you have guilt for attempting to** *bother* **the Almighty with**
17   **a non-emergency prayer, press three.** *(The ACTOR thinks for*
18   *a second. Beep.)* **Hello, you have reached Heaven's Hotline,**
19   **enabling you to speak to the Almighty himself. Press one**
20   **for ...** *(Beep)* **You have chosen the Standard Prayer Hotline.**
21   **Please speak clearly after the tone to record your message.**
22   *(A different beep is heard.)*
23   **ACTOR:** Uh ... hi! I would like to ask God if he would ...
24   *(Clears throat.)* **You know, really ... like ... What I mean to**
25   **say is ...** *(Beep)*
26   **VOICE: I'm sorry, this line does not accept babbling. Please**
27   **state your request clearly.**
28   **ACTOR:** *(Clears throat.)* **Well, I just wanted to ask God if he'd**
29   **be with my Mom as she's having surgery ...** *(Beep)*
30   **VOICE: Thank you for calling Heaven's Hotline. Your prayer**
31   **will be processed in order of its importance with the rest**
32   **of the universe. You can expect long delays. Thank you,**
33   **and have a nice day.** *(Click.)*
34   **ACTOR: Man, I can't believe it! Why do I even bother?** *(The*
35   *ACTOR storms Off-stage. SATAN enters. He is wearing a*

1   *headset and chuckling.)*
2   **SATAN: This is just too easy!** *(Speaks into his headset as he exits.)*
3   **Hello, this is Heaven's Hotline. Press one for English, two**
4   **for Spanish, and three for tongues.**

An Incentive to Give

Theme: Giving, stewardship.

**Scripture
References:** Acts 4:32-37, Acts 5:1-11

Synopsis: A couple in the early Christian era plan to impress their friends by lying about their gift to the church. After all, no one would know, right?

Cast: TAMRA
EDWARD
BETSY

Costumes: Biblical robes.

Props: Fake coins and other accessories (necklaces, other jewelry), a bronze baby bootie, and two boxes.

Setting: In the living room, early Christian era. You will need a table and chair.

1   (*TAMRA sits at a table Center Stage sorting coins and other*
2   *possessions. EDWARD's voice is heard Off-stage.*)
3   EDWARD: Tamra, I'm home!
4   TAMRA: I'm in the living room. (*EDWARD enters.*)
5   EDWARD: What are you doing?
6   TAMRA: I'm getting all our earthly possessions together to
7   give to the church.
8   EDWARD: Don't you think you're going a little overboard?
9   TAMRA: All the believers are doing what they can and
10   sharing with one another. Peter's organizing the entire
11   thing so that no one will be in need.
12 EDWARD: Wait a minute, what's this? (*Looks inside a small box*
13   *and pulls out a handful of coins.*) My Caesar coin collection!
14 TAMRA: You know what the Master said about "giving to
15   Caesar what belongs to Caesar." Besides, it'll help feed
16   the poor.
17 EDWARD: But they'll consume in one hour what took me a
18   lifetime to collect! (*Looks around the table.*) Oh man, that's
19   my bronzed baby bootie!
20 TAMRA: Think of the blessings we'll receive. People are
21   sharing as though we are all one family. Even the
22   disciples.
23 EDWARD: You're talking about twelve poor fishermen. It's
24   not like *they* had a lot to begin with.
25 TAMRA: Barnabas is one of the richest men among the
26   followers of Jesus, and he just sold a large portion of land
27   and gave it to the church.
28 EDWARD: Really? Well, that certainly makes us look bad.
29   (*Pause*) Tell you what. We could sell this stuff and keep
30   half the profits for ourselves. They'll think we gave all of
31   it.
32 TAMRA: But that would be dishonest!
33 EDWARD: Look, we still have a lifestyle to maintain. Do you
34   want to give up your designer robes? Your weekly
35   manicures? Our country club membership?

1   TAMRA: I didn't think of that.

2   EDWARD: No one has to know we didn't give all of it.

3   TAMRA: I suppose it would be a good idea. No one has to

4   know.

5   BETSY: *(Runs in.)* **Tamra, Edward, guess what? Ananias and**

6   **Sapphira are dead!**

7   **TAMRA and EDWARD:** *(Together)* **What?**

8   BETSY: **Yeah. They lied about what they gave to the church, so**

9   **the Lord struck them down.** *(TAMRA and EDWARD look at*

10   *each other in horror, then immediately sweep all their possessions*

11   *into one box.)*

12   TAMRA: **Is that all of it?**

13   EDWARD: **Every last coin.**

14   BETSY: *(To audience)* **The Lord loves a cheerful giver.**

It Doesn't Add Up

Theme: Trusting God, strength in our weakness.

Scripture Reference: Judges 7

Synopsis: God promised Gideon victory over the Midianites, but his efforts seem a bit unorthodox, if not impossible.

Cast: GIDEON
GENERAL
SOLDIER 1
SOLDIER 2

Costumes: Biblical robes.

Props: None.

Setting: By the well of Herod, overlooking the valley of Moreh. (That's a mouthful. Basically they're on a hill scoping out the enemy.)

1 GENERAL: The troops are positioned and ready for battle,
2   Gideon.
3 GIDEON: Thank you, General. *(Looks out toward the audience.)*
4   How many of our enemies do you think we're facing?
5 GENERAL: *(Sighs as he also looks out across the audience.)* Whew
6   ... thousands! Twenty to forty maybe? They look like a
7   swarm of locusts down there.
8 GIDEON: How are the men doing?
9 GENERAL: Ready to fight at your command, sir.
10 GIDEON: I want you to release any man that doesn't want to
11   fight.
12 GENERAL: Sir?
13 GIDEON: If he has family obligations or is fearful and afraid,
14   he is free to go.
15 GENERAL: But why?
16 GIDEON: The Lord told me that he will win this battle for us.
17   But to show his power, we must decrease our number.
18   God does not want us to claim this victory as our own.
19 GENERAL: As you wish, sir. I'll get right on it. *(GENERAL*
20   *exits. Two SOLDIERS enter.)*
21 SOLDIER 1: Man, I'm thirsty. How about you?
22 SOLDIER 2: I could use a little refreshment. *(Both men kneel*
23   *down to simulate drinking from a river. SOLDIER 1 puts his*
24   *entire face to the ground and pantomimes lapping up the water.*
25   *SOLDIER 2 carefully kneels down, scoops the water in his hands,*
26   *and begins to sip.)*
27 SOLDIER 2: *(Enthusiastic)* Ohhh, tasty! Chills me right down to
28   my toes. *(SOLDIER 1 makes loud gulping sounds, then wipes*
29   *his face with his sleeve. Adds a burp for effect.)*
30 SOLDIER 1: *(Boisterous)* Now that's what I call a fine cold one!
31   *(The GENERAL enters.)*
32 GENERAL: We've lost a large group of people, sir.
33 GIDEON: How many?
34 GENERAL: Twenty-two thousand. We only have ten thousand
35   men remaining.

1   GIDEON: It's still too many. We've got to reduce the number.

2   *(Points to the two SOLDIERS.)* **See those men over there?**

3   GENERAL: Yes, sir.

4   GIDEON: Have all the rest of the men come and drink from

5   that river. The ones that put their face in the water, like

6   that man over there ...

7   GENERAL: We keep for battle.

8   GIDEON: No. We send home.

9   GENERAL: *(Stunned)* What? No, Gideon, please tell me you're

10   joking!

11   GIDEON: The Lord was very specific.

12   GENERAL: But — but that type of soldier we only use as

13   cooks or ... cleaning ladies ... or something. He can barely

14   hold up his own sword, let alone fight the enemy.

15   SOLDIER 2: *(To SOLDIER 1)* Tell me, am I getting a blemish on

16   my cheek? This sun is soooo hard on the complexion.

17   GENERAL: This can't be! This will reduce our numbers to ...

18   *(Starts to count on his fingers.)*

19   GIDEON: Three hundred men.

20   GENERAL: Three hundred men! They'd have to overpower

21   one hundred enemy soldiers each!

22   GIDEON: The Lord has promised victory. He told me so

23   himself. *(Points to SOLDIER 2.)* **Soldier! Prepare for battle.**

24   SOLDIER 2: *(Jumps up.)* Oh, goody! Do I get armor this time?

25   GIDEON: A sword, a trumpet, and a vase.

26   SOLDIER 2: All right! *(To audience)* I can't wait to tell the guys!

27   *(SOLDIER 2 exits.)*

28   GENERAL: Are you sure you're listening to the right voice?

29   GIDEON: *(Puts his arm around the GENERAL.)* **Trust me, my**

30   friend. The Lord will show his strength in our weakness.

31   *(They both exit, leaving SOLDIER 1. He stands and faces the*

32   *audience.)*

33   SOLDIER 1: The next day Gideon gathered his three hundred

34   men, and they surrounded the camps of the Midianites

35   and the Amalekites. Just before dawn Gideon gave the

1   signal, and all the men together blew their trumpets and
2   broke their vases. The noise scared the enemy, and they
3   scattered in all directions. Over the next several days
4   Gideon pursued them and succeeded in defeating the two
5   nations. *(Pause)* Huh ... God *did* deliver his people using
6   only three hundred warriors. Who'da figured that?
7   *(SOLDIER 1 exits.)*

It Was Always the Plan

Theme: Joy and celebration, the Resurrection.

Scripture Reference: Luke 24:25-53

Synopsis: The angels in heaven are sad over the defeat of Jesus on the cross until Gabriel sets the record straight.

Cast: ANGEL 1
ANGEL 2
JORDAN
GABRIEL

Costumes: Angel costumes (optional).

Props: None.

Setting: Heaven.

1   *(Two ANGELS from opposite sides of the stage approach each*
2   *other.)*
3   ANGEL 1: Hi, Jordan. What's going on? No one is singing
4   today.
5   JORDAN: Haven't you heard? Jesus died on the cross.
6   ANGEL 1: No way! How can the Creator of the universe allow
7   himself to be nailed to a cross?
8   JORDAN: That's what I'm trying to figure out. *(ANGEL 2*
9   *enters.)*
10   ANGEL 2: Hi guys, what's going on?
11   ANGEL 1: Jordan just told me that Jesus died.
12   ANGEL 2: No way!
13   JORDAN: It's true.
14   ANGEL 2: Maybe you were mistaken. Maybe he jumped down
15   at the last minute — you know, to prove he's God.
16   JORDAN: Gabriel told me they buried him in a tomb.
17   ANGEL 1: *(Gasps.)* No!
18   ANGEL 2: It can't be true.
19   ANGEL 1: That means ... Satan wins?!
20   ANGEL 2: God's plan for mankind has failed? What happens
21   now?
22   JORDAN: The people can't possibly keep the laws of Moses.
23   They're condemned in their own sinful nature.
24   ANGEL 1: That means no more new angel recruits in heaven.
25   ANGEL 2: We'll have to close the Book of Life.
26   ANGEL 1: Stop orientation meetings ...
27   JORDAN: And lock the pearly gates. *(All sigh.)*
28   ANGEL 1: What does the Father say about all this?
29   JORDAN: He — he turned his back on his own son. Jesus was
30   heard saying, "Father, Father, why have you forsaken
31   me?"
32   ANGEL 1: I never thought I'd see a day where singing and joy
33   stopped in heaven.
34   ANGEL 2: It's so sad. *(GABRIEL enters.)*
35   GABRIEL: Why the long faces?

1 JORDAN: Surely, Gabriel, you of all the angels heard that
2   Jesus was defeated.
3 ANGEL 2: So so sad.
4 GABRIEL: He hasn't been defeated. This was God's plan the
5   whole time.
6 ANGEL 1, ANGEL 2, and JORDAN: *(Together)* It was?!
7 GABRIEL: Sure! The Lamb of God came as the ultimate
8   sacrifice for humankind. Look ... *(Points down the aisle.)*
9   He's taking the keys to the gates of hell, and he's walking
10   out. He's defeated death. He's defeated Satan's hold on
11   man. He is risen!
12 ANGEL 1, ANGEL 2, and JORDAN: *(Together. Joyfully, voices*
13   *overlapping)* He is risen ... He is risen ...
14 JORDAN: Grab the party hats.
15 ANGEL 1: Get the cake!
16 ANGEL 2: Call all the saints together.
17 ANGEL 1, ANGEL 2, and JORDAN: *(Together)* Let's celebrate!
18   *(Congregation sings "Jesus Christ Is Risen Today.")*

Just Another Fish Tale

Theme: Repentance, obeying the Lord's direction.

Scripture Reference: Jonah, 1-3

Synopsis: Two friends discuss a rumor they overheard about a fish swallowing Jonah, then come face to face with the man himself.

Cast: RUPERT
SARAH
JONAH

Costumes: Old Testament robes optional. If possible, Jonah should be dressed in tattered clothing. His hair should be white and standing on end for effect.

Props: Fishing pole.

Sound Effect: Sound of something being spit out.

Setting: On the shore of Nineveh. A chair is optional. You will need some sort of screen or barrier for Jonah to hide behind until the end of the sketch. Or, if the sketch is performed in a church, hiding along the front pew works too.

1   (*RUPERT is sitting at Center Stage, fishing pole in hand.*
2   *SARAH enters.*)
3   SARAH: How's the fishing today?
4   RUPERT: Great! I've caught six already.
5   SARAH: That's wonderful! I'll start preparing the rest of our
6   dinner.
7   RUPERT: OK. I'll be along in a little bit.
8   SARAH: But we've already got more than enough.
9   RUPERT: I know. But I just want one more chance at landing
10   "the big one."
11   SARAH: Why don't you do what most fishermen do and lie
12   about it?
13   RUPERT: Good plan, but no proof.
14   SARAH: You could claim you threw it back in.
15   RUPERT: Speaking of that, did you hear about the sailors who
16   threw a man in the ocean the other day?
17   SARAH: (*Shocked*) No!
18   RUPERT: The sailors down by the dock were telling all about
19   it. They said they ran into one of the worst storms they've
20   ever encountered. In fact, they thought the ship was going
21   to sink.
22   SARAH: They must be talking about that storm we had three
23   days ago.
24   RUPERT: The very same. But they said that one passenger
25   came forward and said he was responsible for the storm.
26   SARAH: (*Skeptical*) How can one man account for the weather?
27   RUPERT: Well … he said he was running away from his God.
28   Said that God wanted him to come here to Nineveh and
29   tell all the people to repent of their wicked ways. He
30   didn't want to come, so he ran away.
31   SARAH: Sounds like a guilty conscience to me.
32   RUPERT: That's what the sailors said. But the man insisted
33   they would all drown unless they threw him in.
34   SARAH: What did they do?
35   RUPERT: At that point it looked like they were all going to

1   drown anyway, so they pitched him overboard.

2   SARAH: How awful!

3   RUPERT: But guess what? As soon as they did that, the storm

4   calmed down immediately and the ship was out of

5   danger.

6   SARAH: Wow.

7   RUPERT: That's not all. They said a giant fish came along and

8   swallowed the man whole.

9   SARAH: *(Looks skeptical.)* Are you sure *they're* not telling a fish

10   story?

11   RUPERT: They all swear it's true.

12   SARAH: I don't believe it.

13   RUPERT: Why not?

14   SARAH: It's too weird! I mean, *if* God was that powerful, even

15   I would repent and follow him. But he sounds more

16   vengeful than merciful to me.

17   RUPERT: *(Pulls on line.)* **Whoa!**

18   SARAH: What is it?

19   RUPERT: I got a fish! *(Struggles for a second.)* It's a big one!

20   SARAH: *(Looks out.)* It's a whale!

21   RUPERT: Really? Did you see it jump?

22   SARAH: No, it's coming right at us! *(RUPERT drops his pole and*

23   *they both back away, looking stunned. A loud spewing sound is*

24   *heard, and JONAH comes rolling out from behind a barrier. He*

25   *stands, brushes himself off, then sees SARAH and RUPERT and*

26   *raises his arms in the air.)*

27   JONAH: *Repent!*

28   SARAH: Wh-what?

29   JONAH: Do you want this to happen to you? *(Both frantically*

30   *shake their heads.)* Do you believe God is the one true God?

31   *(Both frantically nod their heads.)* Then tell the village I'm

32   coming through, and they'd better be on their knees

33   praying.

34   RUPERT: We will, we will. We'll spread the news right now!

35   *(Both exit quickly, leaving JONAH standing.)*

1   JONAH: And get me some cooked food. I've been eating sushi
2   for three solid days. *(Turns to audience.)* And it wasn't
3   pretty.

The Life Preserver

Theme: Evangelizing, end times.

Scripture References: Galatians 3:27 (NKJV), Romans 13:14

Synopsis: A ship is sinking. A Christian tries desperately to convince others to put on Christ. His method is weak until he finds the ingredient that will convince them of the danger they face without the life preserver.

Cast: (Names and gender may be changed. This sketch may also be modified for larger groups of up to sixteen cast members by creating new characters using Alex and Laura's lines.)
LAURA
ALEX
CHRISTIAN
TERRY
WAITRESS
VOICE

Costumes: Several life preservers (vests) and a waitress uniform, if available. (A simple apron works well.)

Props: A tray with cold beverages and two mugs.

Setting: Onboard a ship.

1   *(LAURA and ALEX stand at Center Stage. CHRISTIAN stands*
2   *at Stage Right.)*
3   LAURA: Isn't this great? We're so lucky to be aboard the best
4   ship ever built.
5   ALEX: Yeah. They say it can weather any storm. It can even
6   ride out tidal waves!
7   LAURA: Did you notice they even got rid of all the lifeboats?
8   ALEX: We certainly don't need them. They'll only hinder our
9   trip.
10   LAURA: Will you look at that guy over there? He's wearing a
11   life preserver! Talk about lame.
12   ALEX: It's like he's afraid he'll drown or something. What an
13   idiot. I'm going to get some coffee. *(Exits.)*
14   LAURA: *(To CHRISTIAN)* Hey, you!
15   CHRISTIAN: *(Looks around, then points to himself.)* Me?
16   LAURA: Yeah, you. Why are you wearing a life preserver?
17   CHRISTIAN: This is no ordinary life preserver; this is my
18   faith. I've put on the Lord Jesus Christ.
19   LAURA: You look ridiculous.
20   CHRISTIAN: Would you like to try it? It'll make you happy.
21   LAURA: Really?
22   CHRISTIAN: Sure! It'll solve all your problems, fix your
23   marriage, and give you a better life.
24   LAURA: *(Hesitant)* Well, OK, I'll try it. *(She puts on the vest.)* It's
25   kind of bulky, and it's not very comfortable.
26   CHRISTIAN: You'll get used to it, and you'll be glad you have
27   it. *(ALEX enters. He looks LAURA up and down.)*
28   ALEX: What are you doing?
29   LAURA: *(Clearly uncomfortable)* Well, I just thought I'd try it ...
30   ALEX: You look ridiculous. Are you trying to be as weird as
31   the others?
32   LAURA: Well, no, but it's supposed to improve my life ...
33   ALEX: How? By isolating you from your friends? What a jerk.
34   Call me when you return to your senses. *(ALEX exits right.*
35   *WAITRESS enters from left with a tray of beverages.)*

1   WAITRESS: Oh sir, you forgot the coffee you ordered. Oops!
2   *(She spills the coffee all over LAURA. Director's note: Please*
3   *make sure this is not actually a hot beverage.)* **I'm so sorry.** *(She*
4   *tries to brush off the coffee.)*
5   LAURA: **Ahhhh! This stupid preserver.** *(She takes off the vest and*
6   *throws it to the ground. CHRISTIAN picks it up.)* **You said this**
7   **would make me happy. So far I've faced persecution,**
8   **ridicule, and hardship. I'm never going to wear it again!**
9   *(She storms off, leaving a stunned CHRISTIAN standing Center*
10   *Stage. WAITRESS also exits, still apologizing.)*
11   VOICE: **Attention, passengers. There's been an explosion in**
12   **the engine room. Please make preparations to abandon**
13   **ship.**
14   CHRISTIAN: **Abandon ship? There are no lifeboats! I've got to**
15   **warn everyone.** *(Goes to ALEX, who has obtained coffee*
16   *elsewhere and appears to be casually watching a game Off-stage.)*
17   **Why are you standing there? Didn't you hear what the**
18   **Captain said?**
19   ALEX: **Hmmmm? Can't hear a thing. This has been an intense**
20   **shuffleboard competition.**
21   CHRISTIAN: **Life as we know it on this ship is coming to an**
22   **end.** *(Holds out the life vest.)* **Please. Put on the Lord Jesus**
23   **Christ.**
24   ALEX: **I really don't believe in him, and I'm quite happy where**
25   **I am, thanks.**
26   CHRISTIAN: **Please, put on the life preserver. It's better than**
27   **the game!** *(ALEX gives no response, and CHRISTIAN realizes*
28   *what a weak statement that was. He sees TERRY enter across the*
29   *stage.)* **How about you? Won't you put on the life**
30   **preserver? It's a free gift.**
31   TERRY: **Thanks, but I really don't think I need it.**
32   CHRISTIAN: **But didn't you hear the Captain call for everyone**
33   **to abandon ship? Without it, you'll perish!**
34   TERRY: **I find that hard to believe. Besides, God is love. He**
35   **won't let anything happen to good people.**

1   CHRISTIAN: *(Turns to audience.)* **What do I do? So far I can't**
2   **get people to put on the Lord Jesus Christ. How can I**
3   **warn them of the jump to come?** *(Suddenly has an idea.)* **The**
4   **jump to come!** *(Strolls over to TERRY.)* **OK. Stand there. Let**
5   **the ship explode in flames around you. Glug ... glug.**
6   TERRY: **I beg your pardon?**
7   CHRISTIAN: **You see, if you ignore the fact that this ship is**
8   **going to sink, you're going to find yourself in the water**
9   **without a life preserver. You can't possibly tread water**
10   **long enough for the rescue ship to come. You'll therefore**
11   **give way to the law of gravity, and the current will take**
12   **you under.**
13   TERRY: **Oh, I see what you mean!** *(Takes the vest.)* **Thank you so**
14   **much.** *(ALEX and LAURA enter.)*
15   ALEX: **What are you doing? Don't tell me you bought all that**
16   **malarkey about the ship sinking. Besides, it doesn't fit**
17   **you.**
18   TERRY: **Really? Actually, it's quite comfortable. I really don't**
19   **mind it.**
20   LAURA: **It won't make you happy.**
21   TERRY: **No, but I'm at peace knowing I'm safe.**
22   ALEX: **Your friends won't want to be around you.**
23   TERRY: **Then they weren't really my friends, were they?**
24   LAURA: **It won't save you from the ship sinking.**
25   TERRY: **No, but it'll support me until the rescue ship arrives.**
26   ALEX: *(To CHRISTIAN)* **What have you done? You've ruined**
27   **our friend.**
28   CHRISTIAN: **How about you? Won't you put on the Lord**
29   **Jesus Christ? The waters below are deadly without the**
30   **life preserver.**
31   ALEX: **Thanks, but my friends and I have decided to believe**
32   **the explosion never happened. Come on, Laura.** *(LAURA*
33   *hesitates.)* **Laura?**
34   LAURA: *(Turns to CHRISTIAN.)* **Can I have my life preserver**
35   **back?**

Mirror, Mirror

Theme: Hypocrisy.

Scripture Reference: James 1:23-24

Synopsis: Two fathers watching a ball game quickly learn a lesson on walking the walk.

Cast: JOHN
JASON
VOICE

Props: None.

Setting: A gymnasium. Place two chairs at Center Stage.

Director's Notes: Both fathers talk to each other while continually keeping their eyes on "the game" (over the heads of the audience), with only occasional glances at each other.

1   *(JASON sits on one of the chairs. JOHN enters.)*

2   **JOHN: Hi, Jason. We playing your team today?** *(He sits next to*

3   *him.)*

4   **JASON: Hey, John, how's it going? Yeah, they're warming up**

5   **right now. Where's your son?**

6   **JOHN:** *(Points.)* **Number twenty-two, left forward.**

7   **JASON: Mine's right guard.**

8   **JOHN: He's the smallest one on the court!**

9   **JASON: Yeah, but he's got a three-point shot that'll kill.**

10   **JOHN: They're lining up now for the jump ball.** *(Yells and claps*

11   *his hands.)* **All right, guys, look alive now.** *(Suddenly*

12   *winces.)* **Ooooh, not a good start.**

13   **JASON: I didn't see you at church last Sunday. Everything all**

14   **right?**

15   **JOHN: Yeah. Michael had a game that afternoon, so we went to**

16   **the early service.**

17   **JASON: Pretty interesting sermon, didn't you think?** *(Looks out*

18   *and yells.)* **Hey ref, that was clearly a foul!**

19   **JOHN: Come on, guys, hustle down the court!**

20   **JASON: In fact, did you know I gave the pastor the idea for the**

21   **sermon?**

22   **JOHN:** *(Impressed)* **No way.**

23   **JASON: I'm serious. Last week we sat right here discussing**

24   **sermon topics while our kids played against each other.**

25   **JOHN: How did you come up with a sermon idea?** *(Yells.)* **Hey**

26   **ref, he's clearly walking with the ball. Get some glasses,**

27   **will ya?** *(Back to JASON)* **Where do they get these referees?**

28   **JASON: No clue. Probably just volunteers.**

29   **JOHN: So what were you saying?**

30   **JASON: Well, the pastor and I were noticing how most of these**

31   **parents go to church and learn things like,** *(Raises two*

32   *fingers to quote)* **"Love your fellow man," but then turn on**

33   **each other during basketball games.**

34   **JOHN: The baby in the mirror syndrome.**

35   **JASON: Exactly! James one: twenty-three through twenty-four.**

1   As soon as they leave the church, they totally forget what
2   they were taught.
3   JOHN: Yeah. *(Looks out toward the court.)* **Oh man, that was a**
4   **stupid play.** *(Yells.)* **Come on, guys, use your heads!**
5   JASON: **You should have seen the parents at last week's game.**
6   **What an embarrassment.**
7   JOHN: **Really bad, huh?**
8   JASON: **You would think Christian parents would act a** *little*
9   **more civilized. I mean, what kind of example does that set**
10   **for other people?** *(Yells out.)* **Come on, David, get the ball.**
11   *(Both abruptly stand.)* **Yes!**
12   JOHN: **No, no, no. Get him!** *Mow him down, Mike!*
13   JASON: *(To JOHN)* **Hey, that's my kid!**
14   JOHN: **Well, your kid fouled my kid.**
15   JASON: **He was going for a lay-up.**
16   JOHN: **He** *clearly* **elbowed my kid in the process.**
17   JASON: **What are you talking about? Your kid tripped over his**
18   **own two feet!**
19   JOHN: **Are you implying that my kid is clumsy?**
20   JASON: **So you admit it.**
21   JOHN: **You're a jerk.**
22   JASON: **And you're a horse's backside.**
23   VOICE: *(Off-stage)* **Gentlemen! If you don't settle down, I'm**
24   **going to evict you from the game. Let's set a Christian**
25   **example for our kids.**
26   JASON: **Hey, that's exactly what the Pastor said to me last —**
27   *(Eyes open wide, he realizes what he is saying)* **week.** *(He quickly*
28   *sits down. JOHN follows.)*
29   JOHN: *(Awkward pause)* **So, uh, good sermon, huh?**
30   JASON: **Oh, yeah. Real enlightening.**

The Narrow Way

Theme: Heaven, the Book of Life.

**Scripture
Reference:**   Matthew 7:13-14

Synopsis: Several souls are surprised to learn that earthly efforts, success, and selfish ambitions are not the prerequisite for getting their names in the Book of Life.

Cast: ANGEL
JAKE HOUSTON
KRYSTAL KOOL
RUBY DIAMOND
DOUG NEWBERRY

Props: One table, chair, a large book or clipboard, a sign that says "Pearly Gate Entrance," briefcase, and fake money for Jake.

Setting: The pearly gate entrance in heaven.

1   (*ANGEL sits at a desk. A sign either on the desk or behind the*
2   *ANGEL reads, "Pearly Gate Entrance." JAKE enters.*)
3   JAKE: I knew it, I knew it! I knew I'd make it to this place.
4   ANGEL: Name?
5   JAKE: Big Jake Houston, king of the oil business.
6   ANGEL: (*Looks at his briefcase.*) What's that you have there?
7   JAKE: All my earthly possessions, mostly in large green bills.
8   (*To audience*) Ha! And they said I couldn't take it with me.
9   ANGEL: I'm sorry, but we don't allow currency here.
10 JAKE: What do you mean, you "don't allow it"? This is what
11   I've worked for all my life. (*Holds a handful of money to the*
12   *ANGEL.*) I slept with this under my pillow! When my wife
13   left me, only these green bills comforted me.
14 ANGEL: Perhaps it gave you too much comfort. I don't see
15   your name written in our book.
16 JAKE: WHAT?! That's impossible. I gave to charity.
17 ANGEL: What about that poor man you passed on the street
18   corner each day?
19 JAKE: That doesn't count. He's not a tax deduction.
20 ANGEL: Well, sir, there is a place for you down the road. They
21   do accept earthly possessions, although spontaneous
22   combustion is a problem the first several seconds you
23   arrive.
24 JAKE: Great! Sounds like my kind of place. (*Jake exits as*
25   *KRYSTAL KOOL enters.*)
26 KRYSTAL: Whoa, look at this! I didn't think this place even
27   existed!
28 ANGEL: Name?
29 KRYSTAL: Krystal Kool. (*Looks around.*) This place is totally
30   rad! This is better than a hallucination.
31 ANGEL: I'm sorry, but I don't see your name in our book.
32 KRYSTAL: So what does that mean?
33 ANGEL: It means I can't let you pass through the pearly gates.
34 KRYSTAL: Wow. That is a bummer. So do I just like ... hang
35   here?

1   ANGEL: No. There is a place for you. It's down that road.
2   *(Points.)*
3   KRYSTAL: Oh. OK, that's cool. *(KRYSTAL exits.)*
4   ANGEL: I doubt it. *(Enter RUBY DIAMOND.)* May I help you,
5   ma'am?
6   RUBY: Yes. I'm Ruby Diamond. I believe my name is in that
7   big book of yours.
8   ANGEL: *(Looking)* Ruby ... Diamond ...
9   RUBY: Yes. My husband's name is Clyde Diamond. He'll be
10   expecting me, I'm sure.
11   ANGEL: I have a Clyde Diamond. He entered these gates ten
12   years ago. Nice man, if I recall.
13   RUBY: That's what everyone says, but they didn't have to live
14   with him. He was always turning the thermostat down,
15   even when he *knew* I couldn't *stand* the cold. And he was
16   always wasting his time at the church, never at home
17   where he belonged. In fact, I still want to give him a piece
18   of my mind about the broken screen door he never did get
19   around to fixing, not to mention the ...
20   ANGEL: *(Interrupting)* I'm sorry, Mrs. Diamond, but I don't see
21   your name in our book.
22   RUBY: What? That's absurd. I went to church. I'm a good
23   person.
24   ANGEL: Did you have a personal relationship with Jesus?
25   RUBY: I had enough troubles with one man in my life. Why
26   would I complicate it with two?
27   ANGEL: I'm sorry, ma'am, but I can't grant you admission.
28   RUBY: Well! I've never been so insulted in my life! I want to
29   speak to someone about this immediately.
30   ANGEL: There is a place for you just down the road, and I
31   believe they even encourage complaining. They may not
32   do anything about it, but they do encourage it.
33   RUBY: Very well, then. They just better have adequate heating
34   and ventilation, that's all I can say. *(RUBY exits.)*
35   ANGEL: No problem there. *(Enter DOUG NEWBERRY)* May I

1   help you, sir?
2   DOUG: My name is Doug Newberry. I don't suppose my
3   name's in your book there?
4   ANGEL: *(Looking)* Newberry?
5   DOUG: Yes. But I've got to warn you, I haven't led the best life.
6   I've made a lot of mistakes ... I've had a lot of failures, too.
7   But through it all, my relationship with Jesus has gotten
8   stronger, so I thought he would remember me.
9   ANGEL: Yes, Mr. Newberry. *(Points at book.)* Your name is right
10   here. Please enter the pearly gates.
11   DOUG: Thank you.
12   ANGEL: It's strange, but my book says you should have been
13   here a month ago.
14   DOUG: Yes. I'm sorry I'm late. I was on life support.

No Apologies

Theme: Integrity, honor, Father's Day.

Scripture References: Proverbs 22:6, Deuteronomy 11:19

Synopsis: A father is interrogated for his questionable child-rearing techniques. Will he crack under the pressure?

Cast: VOICE (Individual is not seen)
MAN
FIRST GUARD
SECOND GUARD

Costumes: Dark suits and sunglasses for the guards.

Props: Large hand-held flashlights.

Setting: Interrogation room. Place a chair at Center Stage.

1   *(As a MAN walks across the stage, he is stopped by two*
2   *GUARDS dressed in dark suits and sunglasses. A VOICE is*
3   *heard over an intercom.)*
4   VOICE: *(Commanding)* **Stop right there, please.**
5   MAN: **Who's there?**
6   VOICE: **Sit down.** *(The two GUARDS direct him toward the chair.)*
7   MAN: **Why am I here?**
8   VOICE: **We'll be the ones to ask the questions.** *(The two*
9   *GUARDS take out large flashlights and shine them on the MAN*
10   *in the chair. He reacts by wincing and temporarily holding his*
11   *hand up toward his face.)*
12   VOICE: **Is it true that you're responsible for violating child**
13   **labor laws?**
14   MAN: **Excuse me? I don't know what you're talking about!**
15   VOICE: **I'm referring to the questionable activity of 1966.**
16   MAN: **That was over thirty-five years ago!**
17   VOICE: **Irrelevant at this time. Answer the question.**
18   MAN: **Can you be more specific?**
19   VOICE: **On June sixteenth, you subjected your teenage sons to**
20   **an entire weekend of painting the house.**
21   MAN: **They didn't even do that great of a job.**
22   VOICE: **You made them apply four coats.**
23   MAN: **Couldn't help it. The old color kept bleeding through.**
24   VOICE: **The job would have been completed in half the time if**
25   **you hadn't applied paint thinner and watered it down.**
26   MAN: **It seemed like a good idea at the time. I thought I could**
27   **save us some money.**
28   VOICE: **We also have evidence of endless accounts of hard**
29   **physical labor involving ground work along the place of**
30   **residence.**
31   MAN: **Mowing the lawn and pulling weeds builds character.**
32   VOICE: **You make no apologies for your actions?**
33   MAN: *(Crosses arms.)* **Nope.**
34   VOICE: **What about the accusation of cruelty to animals? You**
35   **apparently self-neutered your own cat!**

1   MAN: It only took a piece of string, and it saved us thirty-five
2   dollars. Of course, the cat would never come around me
3   after that.
4   VOICE: You threatened to do the same to your sons!
5   MAN: *(Shrugs.)* It kept them in line, didn't it?
6   VOICE: You also —
7   MAN: *(Interrupts.)* Look, I don't claim to be perfect. In fact, I've
8   been known to be downright unreasonable. But I did my
9   best, and I taught my sons to trust God in all things and
10   to be loyal to family and country. Now, is there anything
11   else that needs to be said?
12   FIRST GUARD: *(Turns off light and takes off sunglasses.)* I've got
13   something to say.
14   SECOND GUARD: *(Also turns off light and takes off sunglasses.)*
15   So do I.
16   FIRST and SECOND GUARD: *(To MAN, together)* Thanks,
17   Dad.

No Task Too Small

Theme: Stewardship, personal commitment, service.

Scripture Reference: Exodus 17:8-13

Synopsis: The prophet has reached the end of his physical limitations. Aaron's solution is simple, yet effective.

Cast: REPORTER
MOSES
AARON
HUR

Costumes: Old Testament head coverings for Moses, Aaron, and Hur.

Props: Microphone for the Reporter (may be pantomimed).

Setting: On top of a mountain.

1　*(As the sketch opens, MOSES is standing Center Stage, arms*
2　*extended in the air. The REPORTER enters.)*
3　REPORTER: Good evening, and welcome to *Amazing Biblical*
4　*Moments.* Today we take you on a journey to the land of
5　Rephidim, where the Israelites are fighting the Amalek
6　people. From this mountaintop view, we can see that the
7　Israelis clearly have dominance over this battle. *(MOSES*
8　*drops his arms.)* Wait a minute ... Now the Amalek people
9　are taking a strong turn. The Israelis are starting to
10　become overwhelmed at the river. *(MOSES raises his*
11　*hands.)* No ... no ... now the Israelis are pushing back the
12　Amalekites. *(MOSES drops his arms in exhaustion.)* Now the
13　Amalekites are advancing ... *(MOSES raises his arms again.)*
14　Now the Israelis ... What in the world is going on?
15　*(MOSES drops his arms and tries to shake the circulation back.*
16　*He tries again to raise them, but they have become too heavy.*
17　*AARON and HUR enter.)*
18　AARON: Hur, come and help me. *(Both AARON and HUR run*
19　*up to MOSES and raise his arms in the air. The REPORTER*
20　*watches what they do, looks out toward the audience at the battle,*
21　*then back toward the three MEN.)*
22　REPORTER: Gentlemen! I couldn't help but notice that what
23　this man does with his arms is a direct correlation to the
24　battle below. Could you comment on this?
25　AARON: Certainly. The Lord told Moses to stand on this
26　mountain so his troops could see him. As long as his arms
27　are raised in prayer, God will use his power to defeat the
28　Amalekites.
29　REPORTER: And if his arms fall to his side?
30　HUR: Then the Amalekites will gain power over our people.
31　REPORTER: Why can't he hold up his arms himself?
32　AARON: My brother Moses has been standing here with his
33　arms up for over four hours. He's exhausted!
34　REPORTER: Your brother, huh? And your name is ...?
35　AARON: Aaron.

1 REPORTER: *(Nods at HUR.)* **And his name?**
2 AARON: Hur.
3 REPORTER: He's a her?
4 AARON: No, Hur's a him.
5 REPORTER: So she's a him.
6 AARON: No. He's a him.
7 REPORTER: Who's a him?
8 AARON: Hur is.
9 REPORTER: Her?
10 AARON: That's right. *(The REPORTER looks toward the audience*
11   *in confusion, then shakes it off and returns to interviewing.)*
12 REPORTER: Now, um ... Moses? What makes you so special
13   that God would deliver your people to victory simply by
14   the elevation of your arms?
15 HUR: He's a prophet. God works many miracles through him.
16 REPORTER: A prophet, huh? Tell me, Aaron, what do you do?
17 AARON: I am chief priest of the people and spokesman for
18   Moses.
19 REPORTER: Why a spokesman?
20 AARON: He tends to be slow of tongue. We don't want any
21   misquotes, especially by reporters.
22 REPORTER: OK. It seems to me, Aaron, that you are also a
23   very important person. Tell me, why not delegate this task
24   to someone of less significance?
25 AARON: Oh, I have lots of helpers.
26 REPORTER: Like who, for example?
27 AARON: *(Nods at HUR.)* Hur.
28 REPORTER: *(Looks at audience.)* I'm not even going there again.
29 AARON: Besides, what could be more important than helping
30   God's chosen?
31 REPORTER: There must be other ways to assist him.
32 HUR: Oh, there is! We support by prayers and giving. We
33   support by teaching God's word to our children. No task
34   is too small when God calls us to service.
35 REPORTER: In other words, you get involved!

1   HUR: Exactly!
2   REPORTER: *(To audience)* **There you have it, ladies and**
3   **gentlemen. Support and participation at its finest. Join us**
4   **next week for more** *Amazing Biblical Moments. (Turns*
5   *toward the three MEN.)* **You can put the arms down now. It**
6   **looks like you won.** *(AARON and HUR loosen their hold of*
7   *MOSES, but his arms remain outstretched.)*
8   MOSES: **I'm stuck!** *(AARON and HUR attempt to pull his arms*
9   *down without success. They finally give up and assist him Off-*
10   *stage, REPORTER following.)*

Present Acceptance

Theme: Gift of grace.

Scripture Reference: Ephesians 2:8-9

Synopsis: Several people are presented with the gift of grace. What they do with it brings different results.

Cast: (Can mix male/female roles at your convenience.)
GIVER
KAYLA
TODD
DEBBIE
GARY

Props: Four presents decorated with wrapping and bows, a dollar bill.

Setting: Anywhere. Place a table at Center Stage.

1 *(The sketch begins with the GIVER standing next to the table*
2 *with four nicely wrapped packages. He/she sees three people*
3 *approaching. They are talking to each other and not paying*
4 *attention to the person at the table. The GIVER sees them and*
5 *picks up the packages.)*
6 **GIVER: Hello there. I have something very special for you.**
7 *(The GIVER hands each one a package. They look at each other,*
8 *confused.)*
9 **KAYLA: A present for me? What did I do?**
10 **GIVER: You didn't do anything. It's a free gift.**
11 **TODD: Watch it. I bet there's a catch. He's probably going to**
12 **try to sell us something.**
13 **GIVER: No catch. It's the gift of grace.**
14 **TODD: So?**
15 **GIVER: So your salvation is secured because of this gift.**
16 **TODD: I don't believe it. Nothing is ever free.** *(Starts to hand*
17 *the gift back. DEBBIE stops him.)*
18 **DEBBIE: Todd, don't refuse it. It's heaven! It's eternal rewards!**
19 **You know, angels, pearly gates, golden streets, things like**
20 **that.** *(Reaches in her pocket and pulls out a bill.)* **I'll give you a**
21 **hundred dollars for it.**
22 **GIVER: I don't want you to pay for it. Just accept it.**
23 **KAYLA: What if I clean your house or mow your lawn?**
24 **GIVER: No! You don't have to do** *anything.*
25 **KAYLA: Oh, yes I do. Otherwise, I won't be worthy of this gift.**
26 **GIVER: But that's the point. No one is worthy of this gift.**
27 **DEBBIE: How about five hundred dollars? Will you accept**
28 **that?**
29 **GIVER: Look — I don't want your money, and I don't want**
30 **your time. I just want you to graciously accept these gifts.**
31 **TODD: That's a pretty selfish attitude, don't you think?**
32 **GIVER: Excuse me?**
33 **TODD: We obviously didn't do anything to deserve these**
34 **gifts, so why don't you let us reciprocate in some way?**
35 **GIVER: Because Jesus already paid the price for these gifts. As**

1   long as you hold to your faith in Christ, salvation is yours.

2   TODD: Aha! I knew there was a catch. What's your religion?

3   GIVER: My religion?

4   TODD: You know, your theology. *(GIVER looks confused.)* What

5   do you believe in?

6   GIVER: Jesus. Just Jesus.

7   TODD: That's too simple. It's got to be more complicated than

8   that. *(Tosses back the gift.)* Take your gift. I'll find my own

9   way. *(TODD exits.)*

10   KAYLA: You can have mine too. I just don't feel right about

11   accepting this. If there's anything I can do, like feed the

12   poor or live a more perfect life, just let me know, and I'd

13   be happy to accept it then. *(Hands the gift back and exits.)*

14   DEBBIE: How about a thousand dollars? That's my final offer.

15   GIVER: If you had all the money in the world, you couldn't

16   afford this gift.

17   DEBBIE: Wow. Then I need to get a second job! *(Hands the gift*

18   *back and exits. GARY enters as DEBBIE exits. The GIVER hands*

19   *him a gift.)*

20   GIVER: I have something for you.

21   GARY: For me? What is it?

22   GIVER: It's the gift of grace that secures your salvation.

23   GARY: Really? And you're just giving it to me?

24   GIVER: It's a free gift from Jesus.

25   GARY: That's amazing. Thank you. *(Starts to walk off. The GIVER*

26   *stops him.)*

27   GIVER: Wait a minute. Don't you have any questions about it?

28   GARY: No.

29   GIVER: Don't you want to offer me anything for it?

30   GARY: Didn't you say it was free?

31   GIVER: Yes.

32   GARY: Then ... no.

33   GIVER: Do you understand all the implications associated

34   with that gift?

35   GARY: No.

1 GIVER: Then why are you accepting it?
2 GARY: Just because I didn't do anything for it, doesn't mean
3   I'm stupid enough to reject it. *(Starts to exit.)* **See ya**
4   **around, man.**
5 GIVER: Definitely.

Price of a Prayer

Theme: Prayer, acceptance.

**Scripture
References:**   Hebrews 4:16; John 5:14-15

Synopsis: An angel takes it upon himself to determine what kind of prayers are "acceptable" in heaven.

Cast: ANGEL
ARCHANGEL
FOUR VOICES

Costumes: Angel costumes (or choir robes).

Props: A clipboard and a broom and dustpan.

Setting: Just outside the pearly gates.

1   (*ANGEL paces back and forth with a clipboard, jotting notes as*
2   *prayers come in. VOICES 1, 2, 3, and 4 are heard from Off-stage.*)
3   VOICE 1: Help my family, dear Lord ...
4   VOICE 2: Be with my father while he's away ...
5   VOICE 3: Watch over my grandmother while she's in the
6   hospital ...
7   VOICE 4: Guard and protect us on this trip ...
8   ANGEL: Good. Good. Very good petitions. Pass through the
9   pearly gates.
10   VOICE 1: Please be with us through this difficult time ...
11   VOICE 2: Grant my mother a safe trip as she returns home to
12   us ...
13   VOICE 3: Keep my family safe from harm ...
14   VOICE 4: Thank you, Lord, for all the trees and the birds in the
15   air.
16   ANGEL: (*Continues to pace.*) Very good. Pass through the pearly
17   gates. (*Motions for the prayers to pass through.*)
18   VOICE 1: I pray my boss really suffers for what he did to
19   me ...
20   VOICE 2: Help me hit a home run so I can be the hero of the
21   game ...
22   VOICE 3: Lord, I just *hate* my Aunt Bessie ...
23   VOICE 4: Let this lottery ticket be the big winner ...
24   ANGEL: Whoa! Not good here. Reject. Reject. Divert to the
25   nothingness of space. (*Waves his arms as if detouring prayers*
26   *elsewhere.*)
27   VOICE 1: Change my attitude, Lord ...
28   VOICE 2: Just help me to be the best I can be ...
29   ANGEL: OK, better. Pass through the pearly gates.
30   VOICE 3: The way she criticizes me really makes my blood
31   boil ...
32   VOICE 4: There's got to be a reason to divorce my
33   wife/husband ...
34   ANGEL: No, no, no. Definite rejects. We'll send those out to
35   space as well. (*ARCHANGEL enters.*)

1   ARCHANGEL: Lieutenant!

2   ANGEL: *(Immediately comes to attention and salutes.)* **Sir!**

3   ARCHANGEL: Did I not station you here at the entrance?

4   ANGEL: Yes, sir! And I'd like to add, with pleasure, sir!

5   ARCHANGEL: Trainee, what is your mission?

6   ANGEL: To clean up all debris and rubbish from the area, sir.

7   ARCHANGEL: Uh-huh. *(Pause)* So what are you doing?

8   ANGEL: Categorizing the quality prayers from the junk
9   prayers, sir.

10   ARCHANGEL: Junk prayers?

11   ANGEL: *(Relaxing a bit)* Nonessentials, sir. God is much too
12   busy to bother with trivial things.

13   ARCHANGEL: I see. *(Takes the clipboard and scans it over. Points.)*
14   This little girl asked God to help her find her teddy bear.

15   ANGEL: It's not even real.

16   ARCHANGEL: Help with a skin condition?

17   ANGEL: Too vain.

18   ARCHANGEL: Get a job promotion?

19   ANGEL: Too selfish.

20   ARCHANGEL: Peace on earth?!

21   ANGEL: Too vague. Besides, this guy said that angels don't
22   even exist!

23   ARCHANGEL: *(Reprimanding)* Lieutenant —

24   ANGEL: Hey, he started it!

25   ARCHANGEL: Look. It's not up to you to decide what prayers
26   are acceptable. God wants his people to take *all* their
27   petitions to him.

28   ANGEL: Really?

29   ARCHANGEL: Not only that, he wants them to pray without
30   ceasing, casting their cares, their worries, their praises,
31   and their thanksgivings all on him.

32   ANGEL: But what if the prayer is ridiculous?

33   ARCHANGEL: The beautiful thing about our relationship
34   with the Lord is that he really is interested in every aspect
35   of our lives. What you think is "nonessential," God sees

1   as valuable.
2   ANGEL: So he wants all the prayers to pass through?
3   ARCHANGEL: Every thought and every word.
4   ANGEL: But I'm in charge of cleaning rubbish and debris!
5   ARCHANGEL: *(Pulls out a broom and dustpan.)* **Don't forget to**
6   **mop the golden streets when you're through!** *(Both exit.)*

A Psychological Dilemma

Theme: Easter, the Resurrection.

Scripture References: Matthew 27 - 28

Synopsis: A patient explains the extraordinary events of Easter to his psychiatrist.

Cast: DR. FRAUD
JOSIAH

Props: Clipboard, pen, and business card.

Setting: A doctor's office. You will need one couch (or three chairs placed together) and one chair for the doctor.

1	*(JOSIAH lies on a couch Center Stage. DR. FRAUD sits beside*
2	*him, clipboard and pen in hand.)*
3	JOSIAH: I'm telling you, Doctor Fraud, there are things that
4	have been happening that are really spooky.
5	DR. FRAUD: Tell me about it. *(Takes notes on clipboard.)*
6	JOSIAH: To start with, there was this prophet that all the
7	people seemed to like. He was healing people,
8	encouraging them, telling them how wonderful heaven
9	would be … You know, stuff like that.
10	DR. FRAUD: And you were jealous of his popularity. A
11	common reaction for those who seek the admiration of
12	others.
13	JOSIAH: No, it's not that. In fact, I was one of many who
14	followed him to hear his teachings.
15	DR. FRAUD: Go on.
16	JOSIAH: Then one day, without warning, the crowd turned on
17	him. They made all kinds of accusations. Pilate stood
18	Jesus and this — this *criminal* before the people and told
19	them to choose which one they wanted to crucify.
20	DR. FRAUD: And this decision caused you to suffer. That's a
21	common malady that stems from a psychological fear of
22	making the wrong choice. It's called "decidophobia."
23	*(Decide-o-phobia)*
24	JOSIAH: No. In fact, I kept shouting for Jesus to be set free
25	instead of Barabbas, but someone came and hit me across
26	the face so I'd be quiet. The entire crowd turned against
27	Jesus and shouted for Barabbas to be set free.
28	DR. FRAUD: Hmmm. You may have "ponophobia." *(Pon-o-*
29	*phobia)* It's the fear of experiencing great physical harm
30	and pain.
31	JOSIAH: The only fear I had at the time was the fear of being
32	stoned by the same crowd who wanted Jesus crucified.
33	Just a few days earlier we were all happy and communing
34	together when all of a sudden, just like that, *(Snaps fingers)*
35	I was alone.

1   DR. FRAUD: So now you have feelings of isolation and
2   depression following an acute manic experience.
3   JOSIAH: Everyone abandoned Jesus — even his disciples.
4   Well … except John. He stood by him the entire time he
5   was crucified.
6   DR. FRAUD: And where were you?
7   JOSIAH: I was standing on a hillside approximately fifty
8   yards away from any Roman soldiers.
9   DR. FRAUD: Why didn't you stand with that disciple?
10   JOSIAH: Are you kidding me? The Sanhedrin was looking for
11   anyone who was a follower of Jesus.
12   DR. FRAUD: I see now. You have "agoraphobia" — the fear of
13   being in a place where escape might be difficult, along
14   with "acute stress disorder" accentuated by the death of a
15   loved one.
16   JOSIAH: What?
17   DR. FRAUD: *(Sighs.)* They got your prophet, and now you're
18   afraid that they're going to get you.
19   JOSIAH: *(Sarcastic)* No kidding, Sherlock.
20   DR. FRAUD: That's *Doctor Fraud* to you. Let's keep this
21   professional, shall we?
22   JOSIAH: OK, I'm sorry. I'm just trying to figure this all out.
23   DR. FRAUD: Go on.
24   JOSIAH: Well … the weather changed suddenly. The sun
25   stopped shining, and it was as dark as the night. Then,
26   when Jesus died, there was a huge earthquake, and one of
27   the worst thunderstorms I've ever seen!
28   DR. FRAUD: Hmmm. Perhaps you have "brontophobia."
29   *(Bronto-phobia)*
30   JOSIAH: What?
31   DR. FRAUD: *(Condescending)* The fear of boom-booms in the
32   sky.
33   JOSIAH: But this wasn't just any storm. The curtain in the
34   temple ripped in two!
35   DR. FRAUD: Not surprising, since there *was* an earthquake.

1 JOSIAH: Do you know how huge the curtain was?
2 DR. FRAUD: I hold with my assessment.
3 JOSIAH: Then something really weird happened. I saw my
4   grandmother walking along main street.
5 DR. FRAUD: What's so strange about that?
6 JOSIAH: She's been dead for twenty years.
7 DR. FRAUD: So now you suffer from hallucinations. That's
8   very common with schizophrenics. *(Skits-o-fren-icks)*
9 JOSIAH: Doc, the entire village saw at least one dead relative
10   walking that day. We can't *all* be hallucinating. (Matthew
11   27:52-53).
12 DR. FRAUD: Hmmm. I may have to treat the whole village.
13   This is a good time to raise my rates.
14 JOSIAH: Then on Sunday morning, the stone was rolled away
15   from Jesus' grave! Rumor has it the soldiers couldn't
16   move.
17 DR. FRAUD: Sounds as though they experienced a temporary
18   catatonic paralysis. I'd better put them on my list and
19   double my fee.
20 JOSIAH: Then people started seeing Jesus all over the place.
21   He was first seen by Mary, then by two men walking to
22   Damascus. All over town there's someone talking about
23   how they've seen him with their own eyes and have
24   actually talked with him.
25 DR. FRAUD: Typical of "shared delusional disorder."
26 JOSIAH: What?
27 DR. FRAUD: It's when a group of people want to believe in
28   something so badly that they all share the same
29   hallucinations about something that can't possibly be
30   real — your dead grandmother, for example.
31 JOSIAH: But even Jesus himself predicted he would rise from
32   the dead. We didn't understand at the time, but it was
33   foretold in the Scriptures.
34 DR. FRAUD: Obviously you've been deceived to the point of
35   losing touch with reality. I recommend weekly scheduled

1   appointments at my office for the rest of your natural life.

2   *(Writes on clipboard.)*

3 JOSIAH: *(Suddenly sits up.)* **Hey, Doctor Fraud, did you see**

4   **that? Jesus just walked past the window. I recognized**

5   **him!**

6 DR. FRAUD: *(Scribbles out data and rewrites.)* **Better make that**

7   **twice a week.**

8 JOSIAH: *(Gets up.)* **No thanks. Jesus is alive … just as he said.**

9   **I'm going to spread the word.**

10 DR. FRAUD: **As long as you're out, do you know a man by the**

11   **name of Judas?**

12 JOSIAH: **I'm familiar with him.**

13 DR. FRAUD: **Good.** *(Hands him a card.)* **He missed Friday's**

14   **appointment. Tell him to come and see me. Poor man.**

15   **We're dealing with the disappointments of hero worship.**

16 JOSIAH: **Um … Doc, I should tell you about Judas. You see,**

17   **he …**

18 DR. FRAUD: *(Waves him off.)* **Just if you see him hanging**

19   **around.**

20 JOSIAH: *(Looks down at card and shrugs.)* **OK.** *(Exits.)*

Putting on the Armor?

Theme: Protecting, defending.

**Scripture
Reference:** Ephesians 6:13-17

Synopsis: Two individuals create a unique visual while describing the armor of God.

Cast: HEIDI
BILL
3-5 non-speaking parts representing DEMONS

Props: A large box with the following items: A ballet tutu, football shoulder pads, fuzzy bunny slippers, Nerf darts, car window shade (cardboard preferable), baseball bat, and bicycle helmet.

Setting: General meeting place.

1   *(HEIDI and BILL are Onstage with the box of props.)*
2   **HEIDI:** Good evening! Tonight Bill and I are going to
3   demonstrate to you all the concept of Ephesians chapter
4   six, verses thirteen to seventeen. *(Reads from manuscript.)*
5   **"Wherefore take unto you the whole armor of God, that ye**
6   **may be able to withstand in the evil day, and having done**
7   **all, to stand."** *(Turns to BILL.)* **Are you ready?**
8   **BILL:** *(Positioned by the large box)* **Ready.**
9   **HEIDI:** *(Continues to quote.)* **"Stand therefore, having your loins**
10   **girt about with truth."** *(BILL reaches into the box, pulls out a*
11   *tutu, and puts it on.)* **Wait just a minute! What is that?!**
12   **BILL:** **It's my girth!**
13   **HEIDI:** **But a girth is like a belt that ties around —**
14   **BILL:** *(Interrupts.)* **You try to find first-century items in a**
15   **twenty-first century world.**
16   **HEIDI:** **How do you expect the people here to believe you're**
17   **surrounded with truth when you're wearing a ridiculous**
18   **tutu?**
19   **BILL:** **Would you be able to stand here looking *this* stupid and**
20   **lie?**
21   **HEIDI:** **I see your point.** *(Continues reading.)* **"Having your loins**
22   **girt about in truth — "** *(Glances at BILL and shakes her head.*
23   *BILL is unaffected by HEIDI's response.)* **"And having on the**
24   **breastplate of righteousness."** *(BILL reaches into the box and*
25   *pulls out football shoulder pads and puts them on.)* **That's a**
26   **breastplate?**
27   **BILL:** **Sure! One hundred percent durable plastic, able to ward**
28   **off big linebackers and sinners.**
29   **HEIDI:** **"And your feet shod with the preparation of the gospel**
30   **of peace."** *(HEIDI does a double take when she sees what BILL*
31   *brings out next.)* **Fuzzy bunny slippers?**
32   **BILL:** **Have you ever seen a violent bunny?**
33   **HEIDI:** **"Above all, taking the shield of faith, wherewith ye**
34   **shall be able to quench all the fiery darts of the wicked."**
35   *(BILL pulls out a car window shade just in time as several cast*

1   *members begin firing Nerf darts at him.)*
2   BILL: Wait a minute — wait a minute — Hold it!
3   HEIDI: What's the matter?
4   BILL: There's something wrong here. All I'm doing is
5   defending myself.
6   HEIDI: What do you mean?
7   BILL: Well, I've got my tutu of truth, my football pads of
8   righteousness, my fuzzy bunny slippers of peace, and my
9   window shade of faith. But I'm getting bombarded by
10   these darts, and I can't do a thing about it.
11   HEIDI: That's because you've got to be able to create a good
12   defense before you can counter an offensive attack.
13   BILL: So I can scare away the enemy?
14   HEIDI: *(Looks at BILL's outfit.)* Or send them away laughing.
15   What you need now is weapons to form a counterattack.
16   Next comes the helmet of salvation. *(BILL puts on a bicycle*
17   *helmet.)* No matter what happens, you have the knowledge
18   of your deliverance as a child of God. No one can ever
19   take that from you. *(BILL nods in approval.)* Then you fight
20   your attackers with the sword of the Spirit — the word of
21   God slicing through their lies. *(BILL takes out a baseball bat.)*
22   HEIDI: That's not a sword!
23   BILL: Haven't you heard of the "No Tolerance" rule in public
24   facilities? *(CREW MEMBERS begin to fire darts, only this time*
25   *BILL blocks with his shield and tries to bat the darts back at*
26   *them.)* Take that, deception! You can't lie to me. I have the
27   truth wrapped around my waist. Take that, violence! My
28   bunnies know the gospel of peace. *(BILL stops abruptly as*
29   *all members surround and advance slowly toward him.)* Uh-oh.
30   HEIDI: What's the matter?
31   BILL: They're all surrounding and advancing on me at the
32   same time.
33   HEIDI: Don't just use your sword — er — bat to fight one dart
34   at a time. Remember, you have the knowledge of
35   salvation in your head plus the Word of God. Use it!

1   **BILL:** *(Thinks for a second, then holds his bat up.)* **In the name of**
2   **Jesus and by the power of his blood, I command you to**
3   **leave. For the Scripture says that "Greater is he that is in**
4   **me, than he that is in the world!"** (1 John 4:4, author's
5   paraphrase). *(All CREW MEMBERS run off, screaming. BILL*
6   *leans on the bat and smiles.)*
7   **HEIDI:** *(To audience)* **And that is how you use your armor.** *(All*
8   *exit.)*

The Right Type of Protection

Theme: Faith, doubt, and spiritual warfare.

**Scripture
References:**   James 1:5-8, 1 Timothy 1:19

Synopsis: Two demons play a deadly game of doubt until they encounter one who doesn't listen to their lies.

Cast: DEMON 1
DEMON 2
DRIVER 1
DRIVER 2
DRIVER 3

Costumes: Red shirts for the Demons.

Props: None.

Setting: On the street.

Note: This is a spoof of a Geiko commercial. The Drivers pantomime driving a car. Once they crash, they freeze in position until the scene is over.

1   *(Two DEMONS stand Center Stage.)*

2   **DEMON 1:** *(Looks Stage Right.)* **Hey. Here comes another**

3   **Christian. Get ready!** *(Both quickly back up. DRIVER 1 enters,*

4   *pantomiming driving. DEMON 2 jumps in front.)*

5   **DEMON 2:** *(Waving his arms)* **Jesus doesn't care about you!**

6   *(DRIVER 1 steers off course and crashes. Both DEMONS cheer*

7   *and do a series of high fives, low fives, elbow fives, and any other*

8   *combination you can think of. Be creative and use lots of energy*

9   *to ham it up.)*

10   **DEMON 1: Great job!**

11   **DEMON 2: It was too easy.**

12   **DEMON 1:** *(Looks Off-stage again.)* **Here comes another one. It's**

13   **my turn.** *(Both back up again. DRIVER 2 enters, "driving."*

14   *DEMON 1 jumps in front, waving his arms.)* **You're not good**

15   **enough to be a Christian!** *(DRIVER 2 swerves and crashes.*

16   *The two DEMONS cheer and go through the same series of high*

17   *fives, low fives, etc.)* **Is this fun or what?!**

18   **DEMON 2: Here comes another. It's my turn.** *(DRIVER 3 enters,*

19   *"driving." DEMON 2 steps out. DEMON 1 sees DRIVER 3.)*

20   **DEMON 1: No, wait!** *(DEMON 2 doesn't hear him.)*

21   **DEMON 2: You have to work for your salvation.** *(DRIVER 3*

22   *keeps coming. DEMON 2 is confused.)* **You're not good**

23   **enough!** *(DRIVER 3 is unaware of DEMON and keeps driving*

24   *forward. DEMON waves his arms.)* **Jesus doesn't care —**

25   *(DRIVER 3 runs over DEMON and exits left, still unaware of*

26   *hitting anything. DEMON 1 goes over to DEMON 2.)*

27   **DEMON 1:** *(Helps him up.)* **Are you OK?**

28   **DEMON 2:** *(Dizzy)* **What happened?**

29   **DEMON 1: It's not your fault. That guy had a powerful**

30   **protection policy.**

31   **DEMON 2: Protection?**

32   **DEMON 1: Yeah. "Jesus Christ Spiritual Life."**

33   **DEMON 2: But I thought they all had that.**

34   **DEMON 1: Yeah, but this one remembered to put on his armor.**

The Risk Takers

Theme: Risk, faith put into action, following Jesus.

**Scripture
Reference:** Mark 1:14-20

Synopsis: Three fishermen discuss the current events of the time: John the Baptist's arrest, and the rise of a teacher by the name of Jesus.

Cast: PETER
ANDREW
ROBERT
JESUS

Costumes: Biblical robes.

Props: A large net (or several nets) and other fishing gear for effect.

Setting: By the sea. Chairs optional.

1   *(Three FISHERMEN sit side by side, washing their nets.)*
2   ROBERT: Did you hear that Herod arrested John the Baptist?
3   ANDREW: Yes, we did. It doesn't make any sense. What did he
4   do that was wrong?
5   PETER: *(Sarcastic)* Well, you know, he *did* tell tax collectors to
6   only collect the money that was due. And don't forget that
7   *awful* message about kindness. There's got to be a capital
8   offense in there somewhere!
9   ROBERT: Make fun if you wish, Peter, but this is serious! I
10   mean, who in all of Galilee hasn't heard him preach? And
11   now that teacher from Nazareth is doing the same thing.
12   ANDREW: His words are good. Haven't you heard him? Even
13   John called him the "Lamb of God."
14   PETER: My brother Andrew was a disciple of John.
15   ROBERT: I wouldn't say that too loud. You better be careful,
16   Andrew. This guy Jesus is actually preaching in the
17   synagogues! That's taking a big risk, if you ask me. At
18   least John had the sense to stay out in the wilderness.
19   ANDREW: But Jesus is different. He speaks with authority.
20   ROBERT: What are you, a follower of Jesus too?
21   ANDREW: No, but I've heard him preach. I've heard of his
22   miracles.
23   ROBERT: Peter, talk some sense into your brother. Do you
24   want to end up in prison like John?
25   ANDREW: John did a lot of good things. He helped people. He
26   brought them to a closer relationship with God.
27   ROBERT: But at what price?
28   PETER: I don't know. Seems to me the rewards would be
29   worth it.
30   ROBERT: What rewards? John failed! He tried to do something
31   good, and it got him arrested.
32   PETER: I would rather do something great for God and fail,
33   than to do nothing and succeed.
34   ROBERT: Not me, man. "Play it safe." That's *my* motto. *(JESUS*
35   *enters.)*

1   **JESUS: Peter, Andrew. Follow me, and I will make you fishers**
2   **of men** (Mark 1:17, author's paraphrase). *(PETER and*
3   *ANDREW look at each other, smile, and immediately drop their*
4   *nets and follow Jesus Off-stage.)*
5   **ROBERT:** *(Shakes his head.)* **They'll be sorry ... mark my words.**
6   **Look at them following after that man when the nets are**
7   **still in need of repair and the boats needs to be scrubbed**
8   **and the fish need to be gutted.** *(Pauses and looks around at*
9   *all the work.)* **I wonder why Jesus didn't ask me?**

A Samson and Delilah Tale

Theme: Deception.

**Scripture
Reference:** Judges 16

Synopsis: "An Adam and Eve Tale" was such a success that another sketch with the same concept was brought to life by popular demand. The dual actions of writing and the pantomime are portrayed at the same time. The Writer is unaware of the characters behind him as they act out in pantomime what he/she creates.

Cast: WRITER
SAMSON
DELILAH
GUARD (Walk–on role)

Costumes: Biblical robes for Samson and Delilah.

Props: Writing tablet and pencil.

Setting: Writer's office. Place a table or desk and a chair On-stage.

1   (*The WRITER enters and sits at a table Stage Right.*)
2   **WRITER: Let's see … What's my assignment this time?** (*Reads*
3   *from a piece of paper.*) **"Create the narrative account of**
4   **Samson and Delilah using your own words." Hmmm …**
5   (*WRITER thinks for a second, then begins to write.*) **Once upon**
6   **a time, there lived a man by the name of Samson.**
7   (*SAMSON enters.*) **He was handsome, he was strong, he**
8   **could fly over buildings with a single bound!** (*He flexes his*
9   *muscles and pretends to fly, but stops abruptly and looks at the*
10 *WRITER, confused. WRITER stops.*) **Oops, wrong story.**
11 (*Thinks.*) **Well, he *was* the "Superman" of the day.**
12 (*SAMSON nods head in agreement.*) **He killed a lion with his**
13 **bare hands.** (*Pretends to be choking a lion.*) **He even defeated**
14 **the Philistines using only a jaw bone from a donkey.**
15 (*Pretends to be fighting an army, then struts in victory.*)
16 **Nothing could defeat him until** (*Pause*) **she came into his**
17 **life one day.** (*DELILAH enters. SAMSON gapes at her.*)
18   **She was beautiful … stunning … gorgeous …** (*She*
19 *sweeps her hair up and poses for the audience. WRITER stops.*)
20 **No, that's not right.** (*She freezes, but looks at WRITER in*
21 *disbelief. WRITER thinks for a second, then resumes writing.*)
22 **She was also very cunning and evil!** (*DELILAH wrings her*
23 *hands and gives an evil smile.*) **She had some sort of magical**
24 **power over Samson. Poor Samson was totally under her**
25 **control.** (*DELILAH motions for SAMSON to come forward,*
26 *backward, up, down. He follows her every hand movement.*) **He**
27 **couldn't defend himself! No. That's not right.** (*Both*
28 *SAMSON and DELILAH freeze and look at WRITER, confused.*
29 *WRITER erases work, thinks for a second, then resumes writing.*)
30 **Let's go back to … Delilah was beautiful.** (*DELILAH*
31 *sweeps her hair up again. SAMSON goes back to gaping.*) **But**
32 **Samson was totally smitten,** (*Hand to his heart, SAMSON*
33 *leans into her*) **consumed in a passion so deep for her that**
34 **he would cut off his right arm to please her.** (*SAMSON*
35 *looks at WRITER in a panic. WRITER stops.*) **No. He wouldn't**

1   **do that.** *(SAMSON shakes his head vehemently. WRITER*
2   *resumes writing.)*
3   **The fact is, Samson had a secret.** *(SAMSON puts his*
4   *finger to his lips as if to say "shhhh.")* **It was a special pact**
5   **between himself and God.** *(He turns his back on DELILAH.)*
6   **His secret was the source of his strength, and Delilah was**
7   **desperate to find out. She yelled.** *(DELILAH pantomimes*
8   *yelling.)* **She threatened. She threw a temper tantrum!**
9   *(DELILAH stomps her feet and pulls at her hair. WRITER raises*
10   *hand.)* **Hold it!** *(Pause. DELILAH freezes mid-tantrum.)* **No.**
11   **That's not what happened.** *(DELILAH and SAMSON look at*
12   *the WRITER. He resumes writing.)*
13   **One day, Delilah brought out** *her* **secret weapon.**
14   *(DELILAH displays an evil grin while rubbing her hands*
15   *together with glee.)* **A strategy so devious, it's been used for**
16   **the fall of mankind since the beginning of time.** *(Pause for*
17   *effect)* **Delilah pouted.** *(Both SAMSON and DELILAH look at*
18   *the WRITER in disbelief.)* **That's right, Delilah pouted.**
19   *(SAMSON looks at DELILAH, DELILAH shrugs, then pouts.)*
20   **Poor Samson didn't have a chance after that. He quickly**
21   **crumbled under the pressure.** *(Ad lib pressure causing*
22   *SAMSON's knees to buckle under.)* **Before you knew it, he**
23   **was singing his secret to Delilah.** *(SAMSON pantomimes*
24   *singing. DELILAH covers her ears in horror. Pause for effect.)*
25   **And since Delilah couldn't cut out his tongue, she cut his**
26   **hair instead.** *(DELILAH forms scissors with her fingers and*
27   *cuts his hair.)* **Instantly, Samson became weak.** *(SAMSON's*
28   *knees buckle.)* **He crashed to the floor.** *(SAMSON drops down.*
29   *WRITER stops writing and says to himself)* **No. He doesn't do**
30   **that.** *(SAMSON gets up and looks at WRITER, confused.*
31   *WRITER erases, thinks for a second, then resumes writing.)* **He**
32   *falls* **to the floor!** *(SAMSON falls to the floor.)* **Hmmm. No ...**
33   **let's go back to "Samson was weak."** *(DELILAH rolls her*
34   *eyes. SAMSON gets up and dusts himself off while glaring at*
35   *WRITER, who stops to think again.)* **Let's see, what else**

1 happened? Gouging out the eyes? Torture? *(SAMSON*
2 *looks at WRITER with panic expression.)* **An entire stadium**
3 **crashing down on him?** *(SAMSON looks up for ceiling to fall*
4 *on him. DELILAH rubs hands in glee.)* **Well, maybe I'll just**
5 **skip that part.** *(SAMSON lets out a sigh. DELILAH looks*
6 *disappointed.)* **The guards come and take Samson away.** *(A*
7 *guard enters and leads SAMSON away. DELILAH snickers and*
8 *does a "victory dance.")* **And since Delilah can't be trusted**
9 **with secret information, she's sent away and never heard**
10 **of again.** *(She freezes and stares at the WRITER in horror.*
11 *GUARD enters again and picks up DELILAH. She is kicking and*
12 *screaming [silent pantomime] the entire time he carries her Off-*
13 *stage. The WRITER looks at his/her paper with satisfaction.)* **The**
14 **end.**

Through Deaf Ears

Theme: Listening, recognizing God's voice.

**Scripture
References:** 1 Samuel 3:1-10, Revelation 3:20

Synopsis: When Eli will not listen to God's voice, God must take other measures.

Cast: ELI
SAMUEL
VOICE OF GOD

Costumes: Old Testament robes

Props: Framed photo of men, plate, cup, two mats.

Setting: In Eli's tent. Place a table and chair at Center Stage.

1   *(ELI is sitting at a table Center Stage with the plate and cup and*
2   *pantomiming eating. A large framed picture is positioned on the*
3   *table next to him.)*
4   **VOICE OF GOD:** *(Off-stage)* **Eli?** *(ELI continues to eat. No*
5   *response.)* **Eli, do you hear me?**
6   **ELI:** *(Calls Off-stage.)* **Samuel, come clear the table.**
7   **SAMUEL:** *(Bounces in from Off-stage. He is eager to please.)* **Are**
8   **you finished, Eli?**
9   **ELI:** **I am.** *(Hands him his plate but keeps his cup.)* **Make sure the**
10 **dishes are cleaned before turning in for the night.**
11 **SAMUEL:** **Yes, sir!** *(SAMUEL takes the plate but accidentally knocks*
12 *over the picture frame. SAMUEL picks it up, and ELI takes it.)*
13 **ELI:** **Careful! Those are my sons!**
14 **SAMUEL:** **I'm sorry, Eli.**
15 **ELI:** **When you get older, you'll understand how important it is**
16 **to sire boys.**
17 **SAMUEL:** **Yes, sir.** *(SAMUEL gathers the rest of the dishes and*
18 *exits.)*
19 **VOICE OF GOD:** *(Off-stage)* **Eli, your sons have done wicked**
20 **things for the last time. I'm —**
21 **ELI:** *(Admiring the picture)* **What a bunch of good-looking men**
22 **they've all turned out to be. If only they would behave**
23 **themselves. Deep inside, they're really good boys.**
24 **VOICE OF GOD:** *(Off-stage)* **Good?! They curse my name, and**
25 **you don't have the backbone to restrain them!**
26 **ELI:** **Samuel, are your chores done?**
27 **SAMUEL:** *(Runs in holding two rolled-up mats.)* **Yes, sir.**
28 **ELI:** **Good. Let's settle in for the night.** *(As SAMUEL unrolls the*
29 *mats and he and ELI lie down on them, the VOICE speaks again.)*
30 **VOICE OF GOD:** *(Off-stage)* **Eli, I'm going to pass judgment on**
31 **your sons.**
32 **ELI:** **Have you said your prayers, Samuel?**
33 **SAMUEL:** **Yes, sir. But when will I start hearing the Lord's**
34 **voice like you do?**
35 **ELI:** **Patience, my prophet-in-training. It's a gift! One must**

1　　have a clear conscience and be pure in thought for the
2　　Lord to speak.
3　VOICE OF GOD: *(Off-stage)* Are your thoughts pure, Eli?
4　ELI: Now go to sleep, Samuel.
5　VOICE OF GOD: *(Off-stage)* Hey! *(Sound of knocking three times*
6　　*synchronizing with ELI jerking his head as though it is the object*
7　　*being knocked.)* Are you listening to me?!
8　ELI: Hmmm. That was a weird twitch. Now I've got a
9　　headache! I'll just dull it with my special tea. *(Takes a sip*
10　　*from his cup.)*
11　VOICE OF GOD: *(Off-stage)* Eli ... *(ELI turns over and lies down*
12　　*on his mat.)* Eli! *(Pause)* How do I get your attention? *(Pause)*
13　　Samuel?
14　SAMUEL: *(Sits up immediately and runs over to ELI.)* Here I am,
15　　Eli.
16　ELI: *(Startled)* What? What are you doing? Go back to bed.
17　SAMUEL: But you called me.
18　ELI: I did not! You had a dream. *(SAMUEL goes back to his mat*
19　　*and lies down.)*
20　VOICE OF GOD: *(Off-stage)* Samuel ... Samuel? *(Again*
21　　*SAMUEL jumps up and runs over to ELI.)*
22　SAMUEL: Here I am, Eli.
23　ELI: *(Irritated)* Why are you waking me up?
24　SAMUEL: But you called me.
25　ELI: I did not. Go back to bed.
26　SAMUEL: I heard you!
27　ELI: Look. Next time you hear voices in the dark, I want you to
28　　say, "Speak, Lord, for your servant hears" (1 Samuel 3:9,
29　　NKJV).
30　SAMUEL: Speak, Lord, for your servant hears.
31　ELI: That's the ticket.
32　SAMUEL: Do you think the Lord is actually trying to talk to
33　　me?
34　ELI: *(Condescending)* Suuure he is. *(SAMUEL smiles and goes back*
35　　*to his mat.)* Like he'd waste his time talking to a boy

1   **instead of his faithful servant.** *(Points at himself, then looks*

2   *up.)* **You know, Lord, it really** *is* **bothering me that I**

3   **haven't heard your voice in a very long time now.**

4   **VOICE OF GOD:** *(Off-stage)* **Are you kidding? I'm** *screaming* **at**

5   **you, and you still won't listen. What do I have to do? Send**

6   **lightning bolts and thunderclouds? I did that last week,**

7   **and you complained about a little rain! The moment I**

8   **mention your evil sons, you shut me down and pretend**

9   **not to —**

10   **ELI:** **This is no good. I can't hear a thing! I'm going to bed.** *(He*

11   *rolls over and goes to sleep.)*

12   **VOICE OF GOD:** *(Off-stage, softer)* **I need a servant who will**

13   **hear me.** *(Pause)* **Samuel?**

14   **SAMUEL:** *(Sits up.)* **Speak, Lord, for your servant hears.**

Under the Microscope

Theme: Judging others.

**Scripture
References:** Job 1-42, Matthew 5:45, Hebrews 13:5

Synopsis: A talk show committee tries to speculate the causes for Job's downfall.

Cast: HOST
PROFESSOR
PHARISEE
PANELIST 1
PANELIST 2
PANELIST 3

Props: Microphone.

Setting: A television talk show. Place three chairs in a row for the Panelists.

1	*(PANELISTS sit Center Stage. The HOST faces the audience,*
2	*microphone in hand.)*
3	HOST: Good evening, and welcome to our show "Under the
4	Microscope," where a select group of panelists will
5	examine the life of a certain individual and basically
6	shred apart his problem. Today we look at the life of a
7	man named Job. Job had it all: a successful ranch that
8	included thousands of camels and sheep, ten healthy
9	children, a loving wife, and the respect and admiration of
10	his neighbors and business associates. Then suddenly
11	one day, it all came to an end. His children were killed in
12	a tragic accident, and thieves stole his livestock and killed
13	his servants. Then to make matters worse, he developed
14	boils and sores all over his body. He's bankrupt, sick, and
15	defeated. *(Turns to PROFESSOR.)* The question has to be
16	asked: Why did so many bad things happen to one
17	person?
18	PROFESSOR: According to *my* calculations, it was only a
19	matter of time. Too many animals, too many inept
20	servants, not enough protection around his borders … All
21	this adds up to eventual disaster.
22	PHARISEE: Besides, it was only logical that bad things would
23	happen to him. He'd been living high on the hog for too
24	many years! Eventually something had to go wrong.
25	PANELIST 1: Did he pay his taxes? This clearly looks like a
26	government takeover to me.
27	HOST: *(Extends microphone to PANELIST 2.)* What's your
28	assessment of the situation?
29	PANELIST 2: *(Shakes his head.)* Tragic. Very tragic. I really feel
30	his pain.
31	PHARISEE: *(To PANELIST 2)* What do you mean, you "feel his
32	pain"? Only bad things happen to bad people. Job clearly
33	has some secret sin he's not owning up to.
34	PANELIST 3: He thinks *he's* got it bad. He should see *my*
35	pitiful life before he starts whining.

1 HOST: Are there any words of encouragement we could
2   extend to a person like Job?
3 PANELIST 2: Let him know things could have been worse.
4 PANELIST 3: What do you mean, "could have"? Tell him it's
5   *going* to get worse.
6 PHARISEE: Look, if he'd just confess whatever he did wrong,
7   he'd feel a lot better.
8 PANELIST 1: Actually, he just needs to confess that all this
9   hardship is not happening to him.
10 PANELIST 2: *(To PANELIST 1)* Are you kidding me?
11 PANELIST 1: It's a simple solution of mind over matter.
12 PROFESSOR: He needs to confess he made an error of
13   judgment with his numbers. Then he can recalculate and
14   start over.
15 PANELIST 3: What do you mean, "start over"? His life *is* over.
16 PHARISEE: Well … at least it can't get any worse.
17 HOST: I don't know about that. Last I heard, his wife was
18   preparing to leave him.
19 PHARISEE: Like I said, it can only improve from here.
20 HOST: We're out of time, but I think we can all agree that if
21   Job was as righteous as he appeared to be, then he
22   wouldn't be in the mess that he's in now. Am I right on
23   that? *(All nod and murmur consent.)* Could it be possible that
24   he really *didn't* do anything to cause his demise? *(All look*
25   *at each other, then shake their heads.)*
26 ALL: *(Ad lib)* Nah … No way … I don't think so.
27 HOST: So in other words, the passage from Matthew five forty
28   five that says that God allows rain to fall on the just as
29   well as the unjust is not true? *(All look at each other,*
30   *confused.)*
31 ALL: *(Ad lib)* Uhh … I don't know … maybe.
32 HOST: How about the passage in Hebrews thirteen five where
33   God speaks to us about being with us even in hard times?
34 PANELIST 1: *(To the others)* I think we've been tricked!
35 HOST: That's right, panel! Case in point: Job proved himself

1   righteous even when he went through hard times. He
2   didn't blame God for his troubles, nor did he blame
3   himself. That's all we've got for today. See you next time
4   on "Under the Microscope!"

Vain Deceptions

Theme: Vanity, conceit, self-righteousness.

**Scripture
References:** Romans 8:20, James 1:26, Psalm 39:11, Ecclesiastes
2:15, 21

Synopsis: Three self-absorbed people can't quite come to terms
with the fact that they've just arrived at hell.

Cast: SATAN
HELPER
RALPH
GLORIA
DONNA

Costumes: Costume for Satan. (A red sweater or shirt is just as
effective.)

Props: Paperwork.

Setting: Hell. Place a podium or small table at Center Stage
(optional).

1   *(SATAN is standing at a podium or other method of higher*
2   *elevation so he towers over the rest of the cast. His HELPER*
3   *enters.)*
4   HELPER: The new tenants have arrived, Your Evilness.
5   SATAN: Excellent! Send them in. *(HELPER motions in a group of*
6   *protesting people — RALPH, DONNA, and GLORIA.)*
7   RALPH: This has got to be a mistake.
8   DONNA: You don't understand. I'm not supposed to be here.
9   GLORIA: Don't we get another chance?
10   SATAN: Welcome, all of you. Allow me to introduce myself.
11   My name is Satan, but you may recognize me as Lucifer,
12   Prince of Darkness, Baal, or a host of other names. Now
13   close your mouths and try not to look so shocked. You're
14   obviously not the brightest crayons in the box. Otherwise,
15   you wouldn't be here.
16   GLORIA: May I have a glass of water?
17   SATAN: My point exactly.
18   RALPH: This isn't right. I spent my entire life studying
19   philosophy, science, religion....
20   SATAN: And I bet you think you're pretty smart. *(Chuckles.)*
21   Vanity. It's my favorite sin.
22   GLORIA: This heat is taking the curl out of my hair! *(Looks at*
23   *hands.)* And look! My acrylic nails are melting!
24   SATAN: Save the whining, princess. Did you think you were
25   too beautiful to be here? Vain, vain, vain.
26   DONNA: But I went to church every week! I taught Sunday
27   school and was loved and respected by all.
28   SATAN: Then when their backs were turned, you talked
29   against everyone in the church and were ultimately
30   responsible for the church splitting up and members
31   losing their faith. *(Turns to HELPER.)* By the way, do we
32   have a reward for her efforts?
33   HELPER: Well, we do have a room with a lovely view over the
34   lake of fire.
35   SATAN: Excellent! You'll be able to watch the swimming

1   events from your window.

2   RALPH: You mean you have people who actually swim across

3   the lake?

4   SATAN: Well ... no. We mostly push them in and watch them

5   scream. It's very entertaining. *(All start to protest. SATAN*

6   *raises his hand.)* Now, now, all of you. You have no one to

7   blame but yourselves.

8   DONNA: You tricked us when we were alive!

9   SATAN: Tricked you? Of course I tricked you, you moron! I'm

10   the father of tricks and lies. I'm happy to say that it didn't

11   take much effort on my part. I simply told Ralph how

12   smart he was; and I told you, Gloria, how beautiful you

13   were; and I told Donna how religious and sanctimonious

14   she was.

15   HELPER: Then we just sat back and let you live off your own

16   delusions and — voila! Here you are!

17   SATAN: Now if you will kindly follow my helper through the

18   brimstone gates, we'll be happy to make the rest of

19   eternity as miserable as possible for you.

20   DONNA: I still don't think this is right.

21   RALPH: *(To HELPER)* How does he know about all this vanity

22   stuff?

23   HELPER: Oh, he's the expert at it. It's what got him kicked out

24   of heaven.

25   RALPH: Really?

26   HELPER: Sure. All this hell stuff started because he thought he

27   could be like God. Then he started recruiting people —

28   about one third of us, as a matter of fact ... *(HELPER's voice*

29   *fades as they exit.)*

30   SATAN: *(Looks over some paperwork.)* Let's see ... what do we

31   have next? Ah yes, a bus load of atheists! *(To audience)* I

32   love surprise homecomings.

Welcome to Stepford Church

Theme: Hypocrisy, seeking God.

Scripture Reference: Isaiah 29:13

Synopsis: An individual finds interesting rules and strange behaviors while visiting a church.

Cast: STEPFORD MEMBER
VISITOR

Costumes: The Visitor should wear casual but nice attire. The Stepford Member should be immaculately dressed. If female, a dress, beads, hair in place, high heels. If male, suit and tie.

Props: None.

Setting: The lobby of Stepford Church.

Note: It's important for the Member to move in a subtle way that looks like a robot. Also, a blank expression and a smile pasted on his/her face at all times adds to the comedic effect.

1   *(STEPFORD MEMBER stands Center Stage. VISITOR*
2   *approaches.)*
3   **MEMBER:** *(Holds out her hand.)* **Thank you for visiting Stepford**
4   **Church. God bless you. Bye-bye.**
5   **VISITOR: Um ... yeah, thanks.** *(Walks away, then stops, looks back*
6   *to say something, but decides against it. Starts to walk away*
7   *again. STEPFORD MEMBER notices the hesitation and catches*
8   *up to VISITOR.)*
9   **MEMBER: Is there something I can help you with? We**
10   **specialize in lost people.**
11   **VISITOR: Well, actually, I've just moved to town, and I'm**
12   **looking for a home church.**
13   **MEMBER: So you're a Christian like me?** *(Pronounced*
14   *"Chrissstian.")*
15   **VISITOR: I am a Christian. But I don't think I'm like you.**
16   **MEMBER: That's perfectly all right. It's not easy to conform to**
17   **the high standards one must maintain as members of this**
18   **church.**
19   **VISITOR: You're telling me. I've never been to a church where**
20   **everyone sat so still during the service.**
21   **MEMBER: There's more opportunity to listen to the Word**
22   **when one is attentive.**
23   **VISITOR: Yeah, but do you think you could blink once in a**
24   **while? You looked like a bunch of robots! It was really**
25   **creepy.**
26   **MEMBER: Sounds to me as though you're not used to a**
27   **structured church service.**
28   **VISITOR: I've been to a lot of churches, and I can say I've felt**
29   **comfortable in most of them as long as they teach the**
30   **Word of God.**
31   **MEMBER: Scripture-based services are important.**
32   **VISITOR: But you guys didn't move, didn't respond to the**
33   **sermon. No nods of agreement, no smiles at the pastor's**
34   **jokes, not even an "amen." I mean, you didn't even bow**
35   **your heads in prayer.**

1   MEMBER: We don't believe in any outward gestures of
2   spirituality. We try not to offend non-believers.
3   VISITOR: Isn't the reason the non-believer comes to church is
4   because he's looking for signs of spirituality? Maybe
5   people who aren't ashamed of showing their allegiance to
6   Christ?
7   MEMBER: Oh, we make that statement with the clothes we
8   wear.
9   VISITOR: Yes, I've noticed you all dress so — *(Hesitates.)*
10   perfect.
11   MEMBER: A well-dressed Christian is a godly Christian.
12   *(Pronounced "Chrissstian.")*
13   VISITOR: How do you figure that?
14   MEMBER: *(Series of head jerks in a robot-type way as she tries to*
15   *process the question.)* A well-dressed Christian is a perfect
16   Christian.
17   VISITOR: Yes, but what is your definition of a perfect
18   Christian?
19   MEMBER: *(More small head jerks as the member processes the*
20   *question.)* Why — a member of Stepford Church, of course.
21   VISITOR: Uh-huh. I think I'll go find a church with people
22   like me.
23   MEMBER: And what kind of church is that?
24   VISITOR: Imperfect. Full of sinners. But with a true heart for
25   seeking God's will.
26   MEMBER: Suit yourself, but you won't find happy people like
27   us. *(Waves to someone Off-stage.)* Welcome to Stepford
28   Church. God bless you. Bye-bye.
29   VISITOR: *(Exits while shaking head.)* Weird!

When God Huffs and Puffs

Theme: The story of Jericho, overconfidence.

**Scripture
Reference:**   Joshua 6:1-20

Synopsis: Two men stand on the walls of Jericho, making fun
of the Israelites.

Cast: AHAB
AKEEM

Costumes: Biblical robes (optional).

Props: A collapsible barrier Center Stage. (We used
Styrofoam blocks that we pulled Off-stage with a
string to simulate a collapse. A curtain folded across
a string works well too. You just simply let go.)

**Sound
Effect:**   Crashing noise.

Setting: At the walls of Jericho.

1   *(Two residents of Jericho, AHAB and AKEEM, stand behind a*
2   *"wall" Center Stage, looking out over the heads of the audience.)*
3   AHAB: Hey, Akeem. What's going on?
4   AKEEM: Just watching the Israelites march around the city.
5   AHAB: Look at them, will you?
6   AKEEM: They just keep going around and around and around
7   and around and around … *(Makes circular motions in the air.)*
8   AKEEM: Incredible, isn't it? How many times so far?
9   AHAB: Seven.
10   AHAB: Seven? Have they done anything else?
11   AKEEM: Nope. They just keep going around and around and
12   around and around. *(Makes circular motions.)*
13   AHAB: But are they saying anything?
14   AKEEM: Nope. They just keep going around and around
15   and … *(AKEEM starts the circular motions again, but AHAB*
16   *grabs his arm.)*
17   AHAB: Stop it! You're making me dizzy. Perhaps this is their
18   evil plan. They're going to drive us nuts watching them.
19   *(Pause)* Why don't they say something?
20   AKEEM: Maybe their tongues have dried up from the desert
21   heat. *(Playfully jabs AHAB in the ribs.)* Perhaps there is a
22   God after all.
23   AHAB: *(Calls out to Israeli army.)* Hey, stupid! Didn't your
24   mothers tell you to stay out of the hot sun?
25   AKEEM: *(Chuckles and joins in.)* What are you going to do?
26   Penetrate our walls with sticks?
27   AHAB: If you think you can take us down, you're downright
28   delusional!
29   AKEEM: No wonder Egypt let you go. You're two cards short
30   of a full deck!
31   AHAB: You're two burritos short of a fiesta!
32   AKEEM: Oh, I like that one.
33   AHAB: Thank you.
34   AKEEM: In the ten-story building of life, yours only goes to
35   the … *(Stops suddenly.)* What is that?!

1   AHAB: Look at them, will you? How arrogant can you be?
2   They're blowing their own horns!
3   AKEEM: Now they're shouting! No matter what they want, we
4   don't let them in. Agree?
5   AHAB: Hey, you're preaching to the choir. Besides, what are
6   they going to do ... huff and puff and blow our walls
7   down? *(The walls in front of them suddenly collapse. A crashing*
8   *noise is heard if possible.)*
9   AHAB and AKEEM: Uh-oh.

Whose You Are

Theme: Belonging, God's family.

Scripture References: Matthew 12:50; Hebrews 2:11-12

Synopsis: An angel interrogates a "new arrival" trying to gain entrance into the pearly gates.

Cast: ANGEL
JESSE

Costumes: Angel costume. (Choir robe works well.)

Props: Clipboard and pencil.

Setting: Heaven. Place a table and chair at Center Stage. Optional: sign that says, "Welcome to the Pearly Gates."

1   (ANGEL sits at a table Center Stage. JESSE enters.)
2   **ANGEL: Welcome to the pearly gates. Name?**
3   **JESSE: Jesse.**
4   **ANGEL:** *(Writes on his clipboard.)* **Date of bodily decease?**
5   **JESSE: Uh ... today?**
6   **ANGEL: There are no "todays" in heaven.**
7   **JESSE: OK.** *(Pauses to think.)* **Then ... recently?**
8   **ANGEL: We've had several "Jesses" today that I've had to turn**
9   **away. Are you sure you're the one whose name is written**
10   **in the Book of Life?**
11   **JESSE:** *(Confident)* **Yes, I'm sure.**
12   **ANGEL: Can you prove it?**
13   **JESSE: I think so.**
14   **ANGEL: Do you have any papers?**
15   **JESSE: I'm told I couldn't take them with me.**
16   **ANGEL: Is there any way you can positively identify yourself?**
17   **JESSE: Um ...** *(Thinks for a second, then points to himself.)* **This is**
18   **me!**
19   **ANGEL: Yeah, that's what they all say. Any identifying marks?**
20   **JESSE: I used to have a cool tattoo on my back, but that was left**
21   **back there as well.**
22   **ANGEL: What about accomplishments during your life?**
23   **JESSE:** *(Hoping to sound encouraging)* **Well, I was a teacher.**
24   **ANGEL: Oh, that's good!** *(Starts to write.)* **Christian school**
25   **teacher.**
26   **JESSE: Actually, I taught in public schools.** *(Exaggerated motions*
27   *as the ANGEL erases/scratches out the information.)*
28   **ANGEL: Church attendance?**
29   **JESSE: Mostly.**
30   **ANGEL: Can you elaborate on that?**
31   **JESSE: Occasionally missed.**
32   **ANGEL:** *(Writes.)* **Rarely missed.**
33   **JESSE: Actually, it was a little more than** *rarely,* **but not as**
34   **much as** *often.*
35   **ANGEL: Purpose for delinquency?**

1   JESSE: Oh, the usual. Not enough sleep the night before,
2   extracurricular activities, general laziness, stuff like that.
3   ANGEL: I see. *(Looks over papers.)* Well, Jesse, with no papers
4   and a meager church attendance, who are you that I
5   should let you pass through the pearly gates?
6   JESSE: Actually, the correct phrase is "whose are you?"
7   ANGEL: Who?
8   JESSE: Not who. *Whose*!
9   ANGEL: What's a whose?
10   JESSE: That's who I am.
11   ANGEL: Who?
12   JESSE: No. *Whose*!
13   ANGEL: I don't understand.
14   JESSE: It's not who I am, but who I belong to.
15   ANGEL: Who is that?
16   JESSE: He's already arrived. *(Points to pearly gates.)*
17   ANGEL: *(Skeptical)* Oh, and you think knowing someone
18   already in there will gain you admission.
19   JESSE: That's right.
20   ANGEL: So who do you know? A relative? A missionary? A
21   *friend*?
22   JESSE: Actually, it's that guy over there.
23   ANGEL: Where? *(Looks around.)*
24   JESSE: Right there! *(Points Off-stage.)* The one who has the
25   holes in his hands.
26   ANGEL: You mean ... you know Jesus?
27   JESSE: More than that. I belong to him.
28   ANGEL: Oh, so that's whose you are!
29   JESSE: That's right.
30   ANGEL: In that case ... *(Sweeps his arm.)* Pass through the pearly
31   gates.
32   JESSE: Thanks. *(JESSE walks past the ANGEL and exits. ANGEL*
33   *turns to audience.)*
34   ANGEL: Wow. It pays to have influential relatives.

Zealous Passion

Theme: Knowing your purpose, a call to service.

Scripture References: Isaiah 26:3; Jeremiah 29:11

Synopsis: A woman is fanatical about her role in the church — much to the detriment of everyone else.

Cast: CARLA
JENNY

Props: None.

Setting: Your local church.

1   (*JENNY enters and addresses the audience.*)
2   JENNY: OK, everyone, listen up. I've been put in charge of
3   making some very necessary changes around here. First
4   thing we're going to do is get rid of the windows and
5   replace them with tinted glass. Next, we need to pull up
6   the old carpet and replace it with a more modern color.
7   While we're at it, let's get rid of the pews and the ...
8   (*CARLA enters while JENNY is talking. She interrupts.*)
9   CARLA: Jenny, what are you doing?
10 JENNY: What does it look like I'm doing? I'm cleaning up the
11   church.
12 CARLA: Cleaning up the church?
13 JENNY: That's right. I'm getting rid of all unnecessary items.
14 CARLA: But I just heard you say you want to get rid of the
15   pews.
16 JENNY: Of course! We can fit more people in the sanctuary
17   that way.
18 CARLA: I don't think that's what the pastor meant by —
19 JENNY: (*Interrupts.*) Speaking of the pastor, do you think he'll
20   be receptive to a change in wardrobe?
21 CARLA: What?
22 JENNY: The outfits he wears are so ancient and drab.
23 CARLA: I don't think —
24 JENNY: And that choir! We've got to fix them too.
25 CARLA: What's wrong with the choir?
26 JENNY: They look waaay too happy when they sing.
27 CARLA: Jenny, what exactly did the pastor ask you to do?
28 JENNY: Actually, it was kind of vague — something about
29   fulfilling my purpose by cleaning up the church.
30 CARLA: I don't think reorganizing the way we do things is
31   what he had in mind.
32 JENNY: I'll tell you one thing, this has turned out to be one
33   tiring job! I don't know if you've noticed, but people are
34   not very receptive to change.
35 CARLA: Amazing. You just now figured that out, huh?

1 JENNY: Take Gertie Gooseberry, for example. She's always
2   wearing those unnecessary fancy dresses to church. I
3   merely suggested she downsize her outfits to fit in with
4   the rest of us.
5 CARLA: I take it she didn't take too kindly to that.
6 JENNY: She called me a few words in some language that I
7   didn't understand, but I'm pretty sure what she said
8   wasn't very spiritual.
9 CARLA: Jenny, you can't possibly be at peace with all you
10   *think* the pastor wants you to do.
11 JENNY: I'm not! I'm stressed, I'm overwhelmed, I'm
12   exhausted!
13 CARLA: Sometimes it's the little jobs that no one notices that
14   are the most important.
15 JENNY: Do you think the pastor had something else in mind
16   when he asked me to clean up the church?
17 CARLA: *(Relieved)* All he really meant for you to do is vacuum
18   the sanctuary after the services.
19 JENNY: That's it?
20 CARLA: That's it.
21 JENNY: Well, vacuuming the sanctuary is an important job too.
22 CARLA: *(Nods)* It is.
23 JENNY: *(Thinks for a second, then perks up.)* Yeah, I can do that
24   job.
25 CARLA: Great! I know everyone — I mean, the pastor will be
26   so happy you've accepted this as your purpose in —
27 JENNY: *(Interrupts CARLA as she addresses the audience again.)* All
28   right, everyone, out of the pews! I've got vacuuming to do.
29   Oh, and from now on, everyone leaves their shoes at the
30   front entrance. I'll have NO mud in this sanctuary.
31   *(JENNY exits while still barking out orders, leaving CARLA*
32   *standing Center Stage shaking her head.)*
33 CARLA: Now if only we can get her to use her talent for good
34   and not evil. *(CARLA exits.)*

Scriptural Index

Theme Index

Scriptural Story Index

About the Author

M. K. Boyle has been writing dramatic sketches for over twenty years. Before obtaining her degree in nursing, she traveled with a local Christian drama company as one of the performers. She soon started writing their material and became encouraged by the reaction of the audience. Her first sketch, "An Adam and Eve Tale," remains a favorite, especially among youth groups. In addition, she has published several collections of sketches for Advent. This is her first book.

She is the drama director at her church, and a member of the Christian Writers' Guild. She lives with her husband Jim and three children, Adam, Jami, and Lauren, in Thornton, Colorado.

Order Form

Meriwether Publishing Ltd.
PO Box 7710
Colorado Springs, CO 80933-7710
Phone: 800-937-5297 Fax: 719-594-9916
Website: www.meriwether.com

Please send me the following books:

_____ **Acting Up in Church #BK-B282** $15.95
by M.K. Boyle
Humorous sketches for worship services

_____ **Worship Sketches 2 Perform #BK-B242** $15.95
by Steven James
A collection of scripts for two actors

_____ **More Worship Sketches 2 Perform #BK-B258** $14.95
by Steven James
A collection of scripts for two actors

_____ **Service with a Smile #BK-B225** $15.95
by Daniel Wray
52 humorous sketches for Sunday worship

_____ **The Human Video Handbook #BK-B289** $15.95
by Kimberlee R. Mendoza
Christian outreach in dramatic movement and music

_____ **Christmas on Stage #BK-B153** $17.95
edited by Theodore O. Zapel
An anthology of Christmas plays for all ages

_____ **More Christmas on Stage #BK-B294** $19.95
edited by Rhonda Wray
Am anthology of royalty-free Christmas plays

**These and other fine Meriwether Publishing books are available at
your local bookstore or direct from the publisher. Prices subject to
change without notice. Check our website or call for current prices.**

Name: _____ e-mail: _____

Organization name: _____

Address: _____

City: _____ State: _____

Zip: _____ Phone: _____

❏ **Check enclosed**

❏ **Visa / MasterCard / Discover / Am. Express #** _____

Signature: _____ Expiration
date: _____ / _____
(required for credit card orders)

Colorado residents: Please add 3% sales tax.
Shipping: Include $3.95 for the first book and 75¢ for each additional book ordered.

❏ *Please send me a copy of your complete catalog of books and plays.*

Order Form

Meriwether Publishing Ltd.
PO Box 7710
Colorado Springs, CO 80933-7710
Phone: 800-937-5297 Fax: 719-594-9916
Website: www.meriwether.com

Please send me the following books:

_____ **Acting Up in Church #BK-B282**   **$15.95**
by M.K. Boyle
Humorous sketches for worship services

_____ **Worship Sketches 2 Perform #BK-B242**   **$15.95**
by Steven James
A collection of scripts for two actors

_____ **More Worship Sketches 2 Perform #BK-B258** **$14.95**
by Steven James
A collection of scripts for two actors

_____ **Service with a Smile #BK-B225**   **$15.95**
by Daniel Wray
52 humorous sketches for Sunday worship

_____ **The Human Video Handbook #BK-B289** **$15.95**
by Kimberlee R. Mendoza
Christian outreach in dramatic movement and music

_____ **Christmas on Stage #BK-B153**   **$17.95**
edited by Theodore O. Zapel
An anthology of Christmas plays for all ages

_____ **More Christmas on Stage #BK-B294**   **$19.95**
edited by Rhonda Wray
Am anthology of royalty-free Christmas plays

These and other fine Meriwether Publishing books are available at your local bookstore or direct from the publisher. Prices subject to change without notice. Check our website or call for current prices.

Name: _____ e-mail: _____

Organization name: _____

Address: _____

City: _____ State: _____

Zip: _____ Phone: _____

❑ **Check enclosed**

❑ **Visa / MasterCard / Discover / Am. Express #** _____

Signature: _____   *Expiration date:* _____ / _____
(required for credit card orders)

Colorado residents: Please add 3% sales tax.
Shipping: Include $3.95 for the first book and 75¢ for each additional book ordered.

❑ *Please send me a copy of your complete catalog of books and plays.*